29/8/24

Hair-Hackle Tying
Techniques & Fly Patterns

Gordon Mackenzie of Redcastle

Hair-Hackle Tying Techniques & Fly Patterns

Gordon Mackenzie of Redcastle

Frank **Amato**

PORTLAND

Dedication

I dedicate this book to fishermen and fly tyers the world over in the hope that it will inspire them to develop techniques and patterns of their own to share with others, thus making fly dressing an ever-expanding art form.

Acknowledgements

Had it not been for my wife Patricia's unending help and encouragement this book may never have been finished. I am eternally grateful to her and her son Michael Witz who sorted out my problems with the computer.

Many world-renowned fly dressers have inspired my fly-tying and bug-making efforts. Veniards' pamphlets initiated me into the fascinating art of fly dressing and the works of the late John Veniard, the late Thomas Clegg, the late A. Courtney Williams, George Grant, Taff Price, Dave Whitlock made me think about the development of patterns and techniques. My thanks to them all and many others for tips on fly-tying. My thanks also to my good friend Mark Bowler editor of the *British Fly Fishing and Fly Tying* magazine for publishing my first article on fly-tying and encouraging me to write more. My grateful thanks to Jim Schollmeyer whose photographs make the book live. And lastly but by no means least my heartfelt thanks to Frank Amato for his wonderful hospitality and to him and his staff especially Kim Koch, Tony Amato and Jerry Hutchinson, for all the hard work they have put in on the book.

Softbound ISBN: 1-57188-268-5 Softbound UPC: 0-66066-00457-4
Spiral Hardbound ISBN: 1-57188-229-4 Spiral Hardbound UPC: 0-66066-00483-3

Frank Amato Publications, Inc.
P.O. Box 82112, Portland, Oregon 97282
(503) 653-8108
Printed in Singapore

1 3 5 7 9 10 8 6 4 2

Contents

Introduction

Very seldom, nowadays, is a new fly-tying technique evolved or a revolutionary fly pattern invented. The development of the "Hairy" series of flies for freshwater and saltwater fly-fishing is no exception.

The basic concept common to all flies, bugs and lures in the series is the substitution of hair, fur, wool or synthetics for the feathers used in the construction of tried-and-tested patterns. Some artistic license must be condoned and I have incorporated a number of my own ideas into the "Hairys".

The main component of all patterns is what I call the "hair hackle". Its re-invention by me came about by chance. While making up an order for Midnight Magic Sea Trout flies I found that, although I tied the required grey speckled mallard feather in by its tip in the conventional way, the hackle fronds splayed all over the place. Further, the thick hackle stalk bulked up the heads making an ugly fly. I gave up on Midnight Magics and turned instead to make up a small order for special nymphs that required a thorax made from fur spun in a dubbing loop. I like the loop method of making dubbed bodies in flies. They look more buggy and the fur quivers when the fly is worked through the water. I finished the nymphs and suddenly thought of using fibres of grey mallard in a dubbing loop to make the hackle. It worked. I used less mallard, could regulate the length of fibres in the "hackle", and best of all the fly's head was small and neat. It is essential to double a dubbing loop hackle as its fibres will then envelope the body and give the fly that pulsating action in water which all species of fish find irresistible.

The major breakthrough in the development of the Hairys came when I was tying Ally's Shrimps on size 10 and 12 trebles. The grey squirrel tail hairs together with the other materials tied in at the front of the fly led to a bulky ugly head. Nothing can be lost by experimenting so I tied the tail and body of the next size 12 Ally's Shrimp, formed a dubbing loop, spread the squirrel tail hair in the first quarter of an inch of this, adjusted the hair to the correct hackle length, and spun the dubbing twister. The resultant "hair hackle" looking like a bottlebrush, was doubled and wrapped around the hook shank. The result was great. The hairs stood out evenly distributed around the body. Two quick snips at each side of the "hackle" and the hair was in place above and below the fly's body. (I now prefer to leave the full hackle as it gives action to the fly). The golden pheasant tippet and orange hackle were added and the head was formed which was small and neat. Looking at the hair on the Ally's, I gave it a tug to see if it would pull out. It didn't and I had found a way of securely attaching slippery squirrel tail hairs to a hook with a mere six or seven turns of thread including that used in the dubbing loop.

I next decided to tie some Spey flies, substituting hair for the traditional heron hackles. They looked good so I included them with an order for Lady Carolines and other traditional Spey flies. Back came a letter saying that the Hairy Speys had more action in the water than their feather counterparts and looked shrimp-like. So Hairy Shrimps followed, then Hairy Salmon Flies, Hairy Waddingtons and Hairy Tube Flies.

The Hairy Shrimps and Hairy Speys have been well received in Canada and U.S.A. where they are used for steelhead. The Hairy Mouse has attracted the attention of bass and trout fishermen. As far as trout flies are concerned the scope for using hair hackles is almost unlimited.

I make no claim for inventing the hair hackle. Over seventy years ago the use of hair in hackles was introduced into fly-tying by Frank Pott and later expanded upon by the "Master Weaver" George Grant. Although their hackles were complicated to fabricate they gave far greater life to flies tied with them than to flies dressed with feather hackles. My method of spinning hair hackles is very similar to that of the "Master Weaver" George Grant, but I think it is slightly easier to do. I hope you will have fun tying Hairys and catch many fish on them. Good luck and tight lines.

Chapter 1

Tools

First, a warning. Don't buy poor-quality tools, they only frustrate you, and make fly-tying a chore rather than one of the most satisfying and pleasurable of occupations. From my experience, and that of other fly-tyers, the only answer is to buy the best equipment you can afford, even if it stretches your finances a bit when buying a vise or pair of scissors. Carefully maintained, good-quality tools will last a lifetime.

The Vise

A robust rotary vise with jaws that can be adjusted to any angle is a must. Always test to see that the jaws hold hooks securely at all times. Rotating jaws allow the spinning of the hair hackle without it being impeded by other materials. I prefer a vise with a clamp to one with a heavy base. The reason is that considerable force is exerted on the tool when packing deer hair and I am always afraid that a free-standing vise on a base, no matter how heavy it is, may move at the wrong time when working on a fly or bug.

Hackle Pliers

Traditionally hackle pliers are used to grip a feather hackle and wind it around the hook shank. When tying the Hairys they can be used to wind the hair hackle, however I find the dubbing twister will do the job perfectly well. Hackle pliers are indispensable for holding hair hackles together if the thread breaks in the dubbing loop. Make sure that the jaws of the hackle pliers close along their full length and have no sharp edges.

Bobbin Holder

This tool holds the spool of thread during tying operations, and you don't waste thread when using it. Further, it accurately controls the binding of thread onto the hook shank, while its weight keeps the bindings tight ensuring the building of a durable fly. The best bobbin holders have a ceramic tube for the thread to run through. Those with metal tubes groove in time causing thread to snap at most inopportune moments. Again, buy the best.

Bobbin Threader

Not only is this tool used to thread bobbin holders, but in a pinch can be used to replace a bulldog clip for holding material before placing it in a dubbing loop. It is often misused to clean out wax from the bobbin holder's tube.

Scissors

Several pairs of scissors are required when working with fibrous material. Heavy-duty ones with curved or straight serrated self-sharpening blades are essential. The serrations on the blades prevent hair and other materials slipping away from the blade's cutting edges. Try to put aside an old pair of scissors for cutting tinsel, wire, and other tough materials. Always buy the best-quality scissors available. It will pay off in the long run.

Hair Stackers

A set of different sizes of hair stackers is useful. Hair stackers are used to even-up the tips of hairs, fibres of fur and synthetics before use. A wide-mouthed stacker is best as it allows hairs room to slide past each other enabling fast evening-up of their tips. Clean untangled hair is important for easy stacking.

The Dubbing Twister

No hair hackles can be made without a dubbing twister. A good one is a heavy brass twirler with hooked stainless steel wire arms. Even better is a turbo one with a ballrace in the head. This one makes spinning of the threads in the dubbing loop easy. The design of the arms in both these twisters braids the thread of the loop locking the hair, wool or other materials tightly in place.

Bulldog Clips

Doctored bulldog clips of various sizes are useful. The grip of the bulldog clip's jaws is enhanced by glueing wide rubber bands onto them. Hairs can be spread out along the jaws, adjusted to length and held tightly before inserting the bunch into the dubbing loop.

Bodkin or Dubbing Needle

This is a needle in a handle which is used for teasing out dubbing, evenly spacing hair in a dubbing loop and applying varnish to the head and other parts of the fly. For myself I fluff up dubbing with a brass-cleaning brush for a .22 calibre rifle. This brush is also useful for cleaning underfur from deer hair, although a fine-toothed dog comb is better as it also aligns the hairs.

Whip-Finishing Tool

Everyone should know how to whip-finish by hand. For years now I have used a small whip-finishing tool which I find quicker than a hand whip-finish. This tool allows me to place the tying thread exactly where I want it on the hook's shank. It is up to individuals which method of whip-finishing they use.

Hair Packers

The best tool I have found for packing deer hair tightly is the Brassie invented by Christopher Helm of Toledo, Ohio. It comes in three sizes and it is best to have all of them as the set allows you to work with any hook size.

Chapter 2
Materials

To fly-dressers, the word "materials" embraces everything that is used in the construction of artificial flies and bugs. The sources for materials are varied and in some cases unusual to say the least. Wild and domestic birds provide a multitude of coloured feathers in various shapes, sorts and sizes; all of which have some use in fly-tying. Animals give us hair, fur, wool and leather of different textures. Further there is seemingly a never-ending flow of synthetic hair, wool, fur, tinsels, ribbons and threads manufactured for purposes other than fly-tying, but these are invaluable for improving the attractiveness of flies to their quarry.

Fly-tyers are inveterate collectors and hoarders of materials. They page through catalogues from material supply houses and browse around haberdashers, wool, craft and model shops in the quest for something new and irresistible to fish. Gamekeepers, hunting and shooting friends, poultry dealers and "road kills" add to the list of suppliers. Keep a lookout for materials such as animal pelts when travelling abroad, especially when visiting a more remote, exotic country. You will be surprised at what you will find. The materials used in tying the Hairys are fairly commonplace and should be found in the storage boxes of most fly-dressers. One thing that must be kept in mind is that when tying Hairys, natural or synthetic hair, fur and wool is exchanged for the feathers required in the original dressings. Thus a Partridge and Orange becomes a Hairy Squirrel and Orange. The brown partridge back feather is replaced with a hair hackle made from the speckled guard hairs of a fox squirrel's pelt. For larger flies, the hairs from the base of a fox squirrel's tail may be used. There is one exception to the use of hair instead of feathers, namely blue jay. (Blue Jay is not legal in the United States. Speckled grey squirrel hair dyed Kingfisher blue is a good substitute.) But even here, if you wish to stick rigidly to hair as an alternative to feathers, grizzly grey rabbit guard hairs or grey fox tail dyed kingfisher blue may be used instead. However there is nothing like a "hair hackle" made from bluejay feather fibres to enhance the heads of Irish Bumbles or the front of Invictas.

The chief source of natural fibres is animal pelts and tails. In most cases pelts have two layers of hair or fur, the longer, stiff and coarser guard hairs and the dense, fine, shorter underfur. The former is used for hackles, tails and wings of flies and the latter mainly for dubbing. Natural or dyed underfur such as that from fox, raccoon, pole cat and opossum is used instead of marabou and soft hackles.

Animal tails and long hair from goats, sheep, llamas, monkeys and bears give us fibres up to 6 inches in length. A complete deer skin provides an abundance of hair of differing length, texture and natural colours. Where possible, natural and dyed hair, fur and wool is best purchased on the skin. This makes for easy storage and the correct amount of fibres can be cut from it when required, Straight cut or cross-cut Zonker strips from rabbit, deer, foxes (especially arctic fox), mink, squirrels, musk rat, beaver, bears, woodchuck, opossum, raccoon and even sheep provide hair and fur on the skin which is tailor-made to be cut off to the correct width for placing in a dubbing loop. There is another use for Zonker strips. When the hide of a cross-cut strip has been pared to 1/32 of an inch it can be wound around the hook shank as a hackle. Although this hair hackle is simple and quick to wind, it gives a bulky body and the density and length of hackle is difficult to regulate. But when the fibres are cut from the skin, they can be adjusted for density and length. Further, fibres spun in a dubbing loop have more life.

Synthetic hair, fur and wool can be used in a dubbing loop in the same way as their natural counterparts. A great deal of experimentation is still to be carried out but one thing is certain, just as hair fibres are more robust than feathers so synthetic fibres are stronger than hair and are just as mobile. You only have to exchange black Angel Hair for dyed black squirrel hair to get a vibrant hair hackle that has a subtle silvery black sheen to it.

To sum up, the uses for which hair, fur, wool and synthetics can be put in hair hackles is almost limitless as will be seen in the following chapters. These materials have many advantages over feathers, some of which are:

1. Hair, fur and synthetic fibres are stronger than feather fibres and do not suffer so much from the ravages of fish's teeth or the huge pressures put on them when casting. Provided the fly is tied correctly and tightly the Hairys should last a lifetime, except if used for pike.

2. Hair hackles can be made sparse or heavy according to the amount and type of material used. The amount of hair required is governed by the circumference of the hook shank or tube being tied. By measuring the diameter of the hook shank and using the formula circumference = πd (where π is a constant (3.1416) and "d" is the diameter of the hook shank), the length of thread required to go once around the hook shank can be worked out. It is best to work in millimetres. (e.g. By applying the above formula, a

hook shank with a diameter of 2mm will require a spun hackle of width 6.29 mm to make 1 turn of hackle around the hook shank).

3. The length of the hairs used in the hackle can be easily regulated. Anything from a 4-inch-long Spey hackle to a 1/4-inch nymph can be formed.

4. Hair fibres stand out around the hook and when stroked back envelope the body giving it a translucent appearance.

5. When hair or fur is correctly spun in the dubbing loop, even slippery squirrel tail fibres will not pull out.

6. Hair and fur fibres have more spring in them than most feather fibres giving a better pulsating action in the water.

7. Synthetic fibres can be incorporated into hair hackles to give fluorescence, sparkle and flash to a fly.

8. There is no bulky buildup of material as occurs when bunches of hair are used for beard hackles or wings.

I cannot stress too strongly the one notable exception to hair's superiority over feathers, namely blue Jay. In my opinion, no hair, fur or feather can be substituted for blue jay hackle. Fibres of blue jay in a dubbing loop hackle improve the look of salmon and trout flies and allow blue jay to be wound around the hook shank without having to prepare the feather's stem for a hackle. It also saves on material.

The only disadvantage to the fly-tyer in using "hair hackles" is that it takes slightly longer to prepare the materials for making them than it does to use feather hackles. Also at first, hair and fur are a bit fiddly to work with. However once you are used to working with hair, fur and synthetics you can revolutionize your fly patterns.

Listed in the tables at the end of this chapter are feathers with their hair, fur, wool or synthetic equivalents.

Hackles
Cock Neck Hackles
The hairs best equated to cock neck hackles come from natural, bleached and dyed (plain dyed colours) and dyed squirrel tails. Spiky guard hairs from bears, mink, badger, fox tails, woodchuck and mongooses all supply suitable stiff hackle fibres. Of all the above, squirrel tails are the cheapest and most readily available. Table 2.1 shows the hair equivalents for cock hackles.
Hen Neck Hackles
The fibres of hen hackles are softer than those of cock hackles. Thus a vast number of softer furs and hairs together with synthetics can be used to imitate them

more closely. Hen hackles are classified under the same nomenclature as cock hackles. See Table 2.2.

Game Bird Hackles
Waterfowl and game birds provide a wide variety of plain, speckled and beautiful multicoloured feathers for fly-tying. Exact equivalents of hair, wool, fur and synthetics are difficult to find. However, allowing a little artistic license, the alternatives listed in Table 2.3 should furnish fly-tyers with reasonable representations of the feathers used in the original dressings. It is always useful to look at the underfur as well as the guard hairs of an animal's pelt. It may be the perfect match for the required feather. For example, underfur from certain brown wild rabbits imitates the snipe's feather used in the Snipe and Purple.

When tying large tube flies, streamers, Waddingtons and sea flies, hair up to 7 inches long is used. This can be selected from bucktail, coyote, goat hair, Icelandic sheep, jackal, llama, monkey, moose mane, Tibetan lamb and yak. It is in large flies and bugs that synthetics come into their own. Unfortunately, barred or speckled synthetic fibres are not readily available.

Synthetic fibres made from acrylic, Antron, Mylars and nylons can all be used for forming "hair hackles". These materials come in several thicknesses and lengths, and in a multitude of colours. The useful synthetics are listed below, but there are many more new ones with which to experiment.

Angel Hair
This is a finely-shredded iridescent metallic Mylar-type material. It is non-absorbent, light in weight and works nicely in the water. It can be used in a dubbing loop to make "hair hackles", adding flash and subtle colour to all types of flies. It is available in 49 colours.

Big Fly Hair
A 10-inch-long slightly translucent non-absorbent fibre. The first 3 inches are crinkly, then the hair tapers to a fine point. It is mainly used in pike and sea flies, and is available in 10 common colours.

FisHair
This translucent synthetic fibre has been around for many years. It is supplied in 20 colours in several thicknesses and lengths. The 70 denier is a good substitute for polar bear.

Fly Fur
A realistic-looking fur made from tapering, fine acrylic fibres. A good lightweight material which is almost indestructible. It has a lively action in the water and is a very good substitute for marabou. The fibres in the dubbing loop should be spaced well apart to give the hackle even

more action. It comes in 20 colours. Always spread the fibres by running a comb through them before inserting them in the dubbing loop.

Lite Brite
Similar to Angel Hair but is slightly broader and stiffer. It has perhaps a little more flash to it. There are 24 colours available.

Mystic or Krystal Wing Fibre
An Antron type of fibre interspersed with very fine strands of pear mylar. It comes in 20 colours. The gold spun into a very sparse hackle makes excellent tails for salmon flies. Run a comb through the hank before using this material in a dubbing loop.

Near Hair or Polar Hair
This is an extra-fine-fibred lustrous hair with a soft action (like marabou) in water. It does not mat and can be coloured with permanent marker pens. It comes in 22 very useful colours.

Super Hair
A soft, crinkled synthetic hair that does not mat or take a set. It has excellent action in the water. It comes in 16 different colours, most of which are useful for sea flies.

There are myriad types of synthetic hairs and furs available and many are the same material under different brand names. In other words, you pays your money and takes your choice.

Table 2.1: Cock Neck Hackles

Feather	Hair, Fur, Wool or Synthetic Equivalents for Feathers
Badger Cock Hackle	Grey squirrel tail with long white tip to hairs and a distinct black bar half way up the hair
Blue Dun Cock Hackle	Grey squirrel tail dyed blue dun
Cock-Y-Bondhu Cock Hackle	Dark pine squirrel tail hairs
Cree Cock Hackle	Red fox tail hairs or light-coloured barred fox squirrel tail
Dark Red/ Brown Cock Hackle	Plain dark brown Russian red squirrel tail
Ginger Cock Hackle	Hairs from the underside of a fox squirrel tail
Greenwell Cock Hackle	Light pine squirrel tail hairs
Grizzly Cock Hackle	Grey fox tail hair or speckled grey mongoose guard hairs
Honey Cock Hackle	Beaver or muskrat
Medium Red/Brown Cock Hackle	Plain light-brown Russian red squirrel tail or black hair from silver fox tail
White Cock Hackle	White fine bucktail, calf tail or short goat hair
Cock Hackles Dyed: Black, blue, claret, green, chartreuse, fiery brown, magenta, olive, pink, purple, red, yellow	Grey squirrel tail dyed if you want light-coloured tips and dark base. Bleached and dyed squirrel tail for hairs of a plain colour

Table 2.2: Hen Neck Hackles

Feather	Hair, Fur, Wool or Synthetic Equivalents for Feathers
Badger Cock Hackle	White-tipped woodchuck body fur
Black Hen Hackle (Natural)	Black body hairs from silver fox, black bear hair or if you want very soft hackles, guard hairs from black rabbit
Dyed Black Hen Hackle	Fox or fin raccoon fur dyed black or black Angel Hair
Blue Dun Hen Hackle	Grey underfur from silver fox or silver-grey mink guard hairs
Cock-Y-Bondhu Hen Hackles	Woodchuck body guard hairs dyed rusty-brown or dark fine squirrel tail
Cream Hen Hackle	Underfur from badger or opossum
Cree Hen Hackle	Hairs selected from a red fox tail
Dark Red/ Brown Hen Hackle	Very dark brown fur from a mink, fin raccoon hair dyed dark brown or brown bear underfur
Ginger Hen Hackle	Dyed ginger arctic fox body fur or underfur from fox squirrel pelt
Greenwell Hen Hackle	Light ginger tipped hairs from pine squirrel
Grizzly Hen Hackle	Speckled grey squirrel hair or in small sizes grizzly grey rabbit guard hairs
Honey Hen Hackle	Bleached beaver hair or arctic fox fur dyed ginger
Light Red Game Hen Hackle	Fox squirrel belly and rump fur, arctic fox fur dyed tan or light brown mink fur
Medium Red/Brown Hen Hackle	Arctic fox dyed fiery brown, fin raccoon dyed brown or Russian red squirrel dyed ginger
White Hen Hackle	Arctic fox body fur or white calf body hair
Hen Hackles Dyed: Blue, claret, green, chartreuse, fiery brown, magenta, olive, pink, purple, red, scarlet, yellow	Dyed arctic fox body fur, dyed polar bear gives translucent colours or Angel Hair which gives shimmering colours

Table 2.3: Water Fowl And Game Birds

Feather	Hair, Fur, Wool or Synthetic Equivalents for Feathers
Coot Body	Iron blue underfur from silver or grey fox body fur
Golden Pheasant Breast	Natural brown bucktail dyed red, grey squirrel tail dyed crimson or for brighter colour grey squirrel tail dyed fluorescent red
Golden Pheasant Rump	Grey squirrel dyed golden olive
Golden Pheasant Crest	Fluorescent yellow mystic synthetic fibres, yellow Antron or goat dyed bright yellow
Golden Pheasant Tippet	Black-tipped polecat, fin raccoon, opossum guard hairs or grey fox tail hairs dyed hot orange
Dyed Goose Wing Feathers	Dyed white bucktail, arctix fox tail or bleached and dyed grey squirrel tail
Grouse Body Feathers	Barred fox squirrel tail dyed ginger
Guineafowl Hackles	Black-tipped grey fox hair. For dyed colours grey or silver fox guard hairs
Blue Jay	No really good equivalent but speckled grey squirrel hair dyed kingfisher blue is a good substitute
Jungle Cock	Black-tipped grey fox hair
Bronze Mallard	Selected hair from natural red or black Russian squirrel tails
Grey Mallard Flank	Hair from the base of a grey squirrel tail or vervet monkey hair

Chapter 3

Preparation of Materials

In all aspects of fly dressing, returning to basic concepts is essential. I would like to stress that the basis of all Hairys is spinning natural or synthetic fibres in a dubbing loop to form a "hair hackle". Spinning fur, wool and guard hairs in a dubbing loop to make fuzzy dubbed bodies on flies has been around for a long time. Although this method of forming bodies is time-consuming the resultant buggy look it produces is attractive to fish and fishermen alike. The "hair hackle" has similar attributes. It envelopes the body making it appear bulky, yet the hackle fibres pulsate giving vibrant lifelike action to the fly as it swims through the water.

It is important in all fly-tying, but especially in production fly tying, to select, prepare and lay out the required materials before starting to tie flies. It saves time, and properly chosen materials will give symmetry to a set of flies. A fly-box containing rows of flies proportionally correct in every way is a delight to behold.

Hair, fur and wool come from animal pelts which makes selection and preparation of materials used in "hair hackles" easy. The first step in material preparation is to cut bunches of hair or fur from the skin or tail, remove unwanted underfur and level the tips of the fibres in a hair stacker. Now, lay out the prepared bunches of hair on the bench in front of you, ready to insert into the waxed thread loop.

A tip for you before going on. If you want to have a wide variety of hair and fur to work with, buy cross-cut or lengthwise-cut Zonker-type strips taken from different animal pelts (e.g. rabbit, mink, all foxes, marmot, squirrel, opossums, woodchuck, raccoon and others). Also animal tails will give you a multitude of different natural and dyed material. Several other benefits are derived from using Zonker strips:

1. The density of fur on a strip is determined by its width. This makes it easier to cut bunches of fur of equal size.

2. The length of fibres required for the "hair hackle" can be adjusted by moving the hairs on the Zonker strip back and forward through the dubbing loop before trapping and cutting off the requisite amount of material.

At this point it is necessary to define the parts of a hook. These are shown below. (Diagram 3.0). The various lengths shown will be used in determining the correct dimensions of tails, hackles and wings of the Hairys, and at which point on the shank they should be placed.

Paramount to the construction of all bugs and flies is a firm foundation. Let us start with this process (Diagram 3.1). Place the hook in the jaws of the vise, making sure that it is securely held by its bend. (Some fly-tyers advocate that the hook point should be covered to prevent the tying thread being caught on it and breaking. I feel that clamping the barb in the vise's jaws may cause cracking at this the hook's weakest point and it breaking at most inopportune moments—usually in the fish's mouth.) Draw off about 6 inches

Diagram 3.0

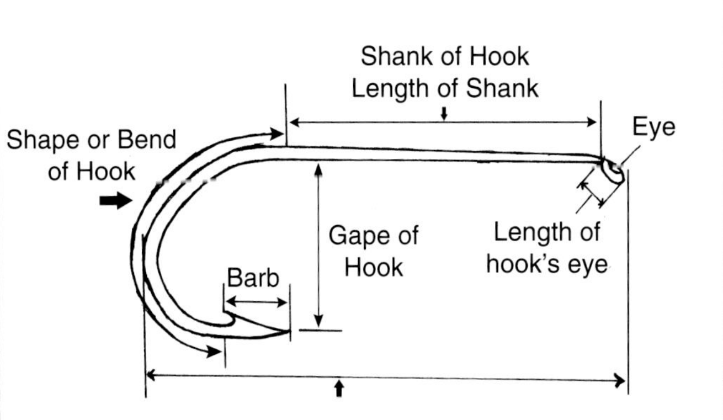

Shank of Hook
Length of Shank

Shape or Bend of Hook

Eye

Gape of Hook

Length of hook's eye

Barb

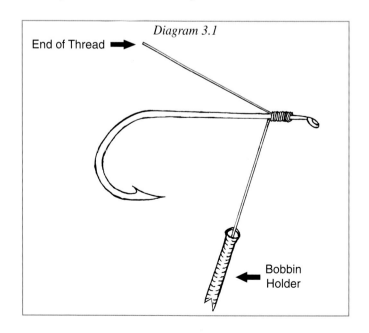

Diagram 3.1

End of Thread ➡

Bobbin Holder ⬅

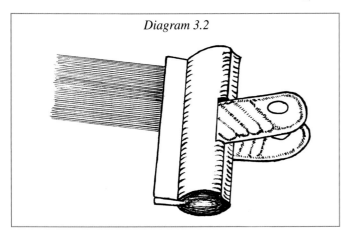

Diagram 3.2

(15cm) of thread through the bobbin holder's tube. Holding thread "A" between the finger and thumb of the left hand, place the thread against the near side of the hook's shank and working back towards the bend, wind a dozen tight turns over the hook shank and thread. Pull end "A" to tighten thread and to bring the coils up against one another. A useful tip: If you pull end "A" sharply towards the hook's eye, it will tighten the thread, pull the coils together and snap off the thread under the coils, forming a very firm foundation on which to tie the rest of the fly. (Do not try this operation when using Kevlar thread.) Now the rest of the fly can be tied.

The core of both spun dubbed bodies and the "hair hackle" is the dubbing loop, so anyone who has used the loop method to create a dubbing brush is halfway there as far as constructing "hair hackles". Initially the best practice and most pleasing results will be attained by using squirrel tail hairs for the "hackle".

Method

Step 1: (Diagrams 3.2 and 3.5). Using a prepared small bundle of squirrel tail hair, spread it out between the jaws of a bulldog clip. The required width of the spread-out hair is determined by the circumference of the hook shank plus any materials wrapped over it, and by the number of hackle turns needed for that type of fly. (Refer back to Chapter 2 and the formula circumference = TTd to work out length of hackle required.) The wider the spread-out hair, the longer will be the hackle. The density of the "hair hackle" depends on how the hair is spread out along the dubbing loop. The closer the hair or fur fibres are together, the more dense will be the "hackle".

Step 2: (Diagrams 3.3 and 3.4.) Form a loop of thread at a point on the hook's shank where you want the "hair hackle". To achieve the loop, draw off 4 to 10 inches of thread from the bobbin holder. Remember, when the loop is twisted, it shortens by up to 1/4 of its length. You must allow for this when determining the width of the "hair hackle" and therefore the length of thread required to form the loop. Wax the thread thoroughly with tacky wax. I use bees' wax. Bring the thread towards you. Place the index finger of the left hand on top of the thread. Double the thread over the finger and back to the point on the shank from where you started. Secure the loop by making 2 turns around the shank. To draw the loop threads together make 1 complete turn of thread around the base of the loop tight up against the hook shank. To lock the loop in place make 2 or 3 turns of thread around the hook shank. A half hitch here will stop any movement.

Step 3: As a precaution, rewax the threads of the dubbing loop.

Step 4: Insert the wire arms of the dubbing twister into the loop. The spring arms of the twister should keep the loop open, enabling you to insert the hairs. I

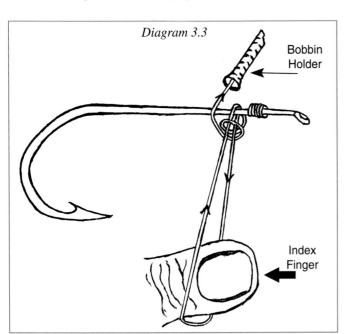

Diagram 3.3

Bobbin Holder

Index Finger

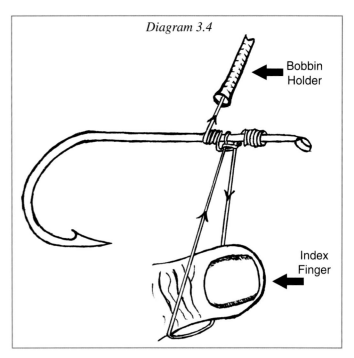

Diagram 3.4

Bobbin Holder

Index Finger

use a turbo dubbing twister as it is heavy and a flick of the ballraced head twists the thread instantly.

Step 5: (Diagrams 3.5). Place the hairs pinched in the bulldog clip between the threads of the dubbing loop, close the index finger and thumb on to the loop threads. Adjust the hair to the length required for the "hackle" and open and remove the bulldog clip. Holding the loop under tension so that the hair will not move or fall out, cut off the hair butts to within 1/16 to 1/8 of an inch from the dubbing loop threads.

Step 6: (Diagrams 3.6, 3.7 and 3.8) Without letting go of the dubbing loop threads and keeping the dubbing twister below the finger and thumb of the left hand spin it clockwise. (Keep the loop with inserted hairs under tension at all times.). Slightly release the pressure of the finger and thumb on the loop allowing the whole system to spin. Still keeping the loop under tension, spin the twister until the fibres stick out like a bottlebrush. You should now have 2 complete circles, a short inner one of butts and a longer outer one of hair points. Double the "hair hackle" and wind it around the shank keeping it as tight as possible against the shank. (Diagrams 3.9 and 3.10). Tie in the "hair hackle with the tying thread. Make 2 turns of thread over the base of the "hackle" in order to make it slope back slightly. The "hackle" should now envelope the body. If more materials are to be tied in, half hitch. If no more materials are required from a small head, whip-finish and varnish it. (Diagram 3.11).

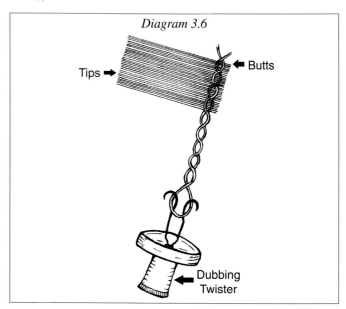

Diagram 3.6

Tips

Butts

Dubbing Twister

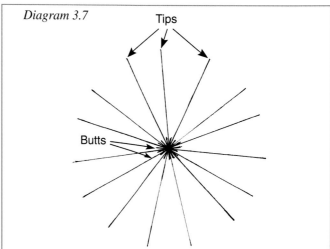

Diagram 3.7

Tips

Butts

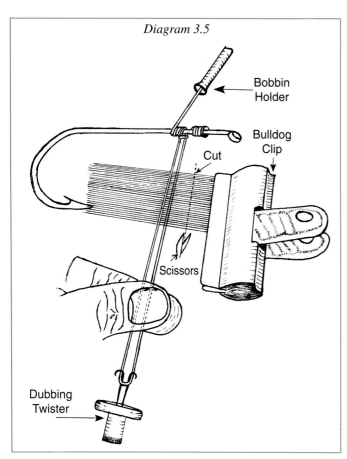

Diagram 3.5

Bobbin Holder

Bulldog Clip

Cut

Scissors

Dubbing Twister

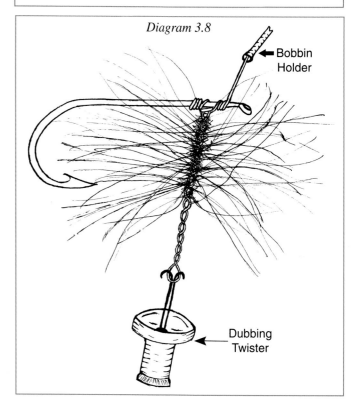

Diagram 3.8

Bobbin Holder

Dubbing Twister

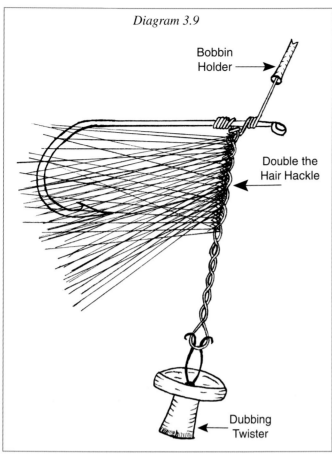

Diagram 3.9

Bobbin Holder

Double the Hair Hackle

Dubbing Twister

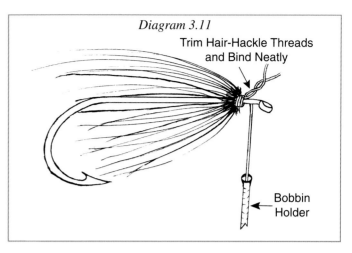

Diagram 3.11

Trim Hair-Hackle Threads and Bind Neatly

Bobbin Holder

Just as dubbing brushes are mechanically formed so "hair hackles" can be preformed using very fine orthodontic or beading wire for the loop. The principles of construction are the same as for forming "hair hackles" with thread on a hook. The processes will be discussed in some detail when dealing with Matuka-style flies and bass bugs in later chapters.

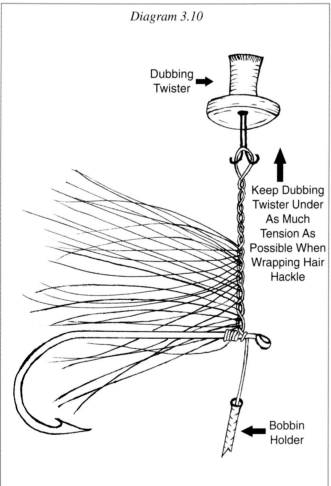

Diagram 3.10

Dubbing Twister

Keep Dubbing Twister Under As Much Tension As Possible When Wrapping Hair Hackle

Bobbin Holder

Chapter 4

Hairy Trout Flies

Fly-dressing is a fascinating artform reaching its pinnacle in the tying of full-dress salmon flies. To attain these heights, the basic principles of fly-tying have to be mastered.

When I took up fly-tying in 1952, introductory books on the subject recommended that the first fly a beginner attempted should be a simple hackle pattern. Things have changed over the years. The study of the feeding habits of fish has shown that the main diet of trout is subsurface aquatic life forms, especially nymphs and larvae. This has given rise to an upsurge in nymph fishing and consequently the development of numerous nymph and larvae patterns. So for the prospective fly-tyer the hackle fly is discarded, and he or she is initiated into the mysteries of fly-dressing by tying a larva pattern of some sort. Following the modern trends, the methods of dressing the Hairys will be introduced by showing the techniques involved in tying pupae and larvae representations. The tying programme will then progress through more complicated patterns until all the basic skills have been covered and Hairy Shrimps and fry patterns can, I hope, be produced by novice and experienced fly-tyers alike.

Many fly patterns especially those representing nymphs and baitfish have to be weighted. This weight allows imitative flies to be presented to feeding fish at a depth where their natural food occurs. It is important that these weighted flies look natural when worked through water. The fly should swim either hook point up, making them almost weedless, or, in the conventional way, hook point down. To achieve this a small keel must be incorporated into the weight needed to make flies sink to the requisite depth. From my experience, flies swimming on their side don't seem to hook as many fish.

The Keel Method of Weighting Flies

Step 1: Place the hook in the vise's jaws.

Step 2: Form a firm thread foundation stretching from 1/4 of the shank's length behind the eye to the hook's bend.

Step 3: Spiral the tying thread forward to a point 3/4 of the shank's length from the eye.

Step 4: (Diagrams 4.0 and 4.1). Tie in lead or copper wire so that it lies along the underside of the hook shank creating the base of a keel. To complete the keel, wrap the wire around itself and the hook shank to where the thread foundation began. Make the keel more prominent by squeezing it with pliers so that 1/2 the keel lies under the shank. This ensures that the hook point rides below the shank. To have the hook point riding up, tie in the wire along the top side of the shank and reverse the dressing.

These processes are used in tying all weighted Hairys. A useful tip: When you have some time on your hands, make up an assortment of weighted hooks and store them for future use.

Having digressed into explaining the Keel method of weighting hooks, it is now time to get down to the business of dressing the Hairys.

A Hairy Larva is one of the easiest of all flies to tie. If fished correctly it is a deadly pattern in both river and lake. By merely changing the body colours, a wide range of very effective nymph type flies can be tied.

◁⧉ **Hairy Cream Larva** ⧉▷

Hook: TMC 2487, Partridge YK4A, Mustad 80250BR, Daiichi 1130, sizes 10-18 wtd.

Thread: Yellow 6/0 or 8/0.

Weight: Copper or lead wire.

Ribbing: Gold wire.

Body: Cream underfur from a woodchuck pelt.

Head: Brown dubbing or black Flashabou dubbing (Angel Hair).

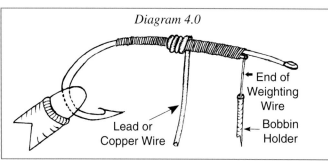

Diagram 4.0

End of Weighting Wire

Lead or Copper Wire

Bobbin Holder

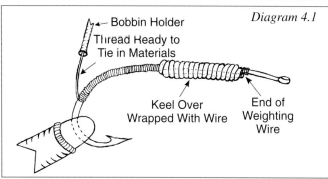

Bobbin Holder
Thread Ready to Tie in Materials

Diagram 4.1

Keel Over Wrapped With Wire

End of Weighting Wire

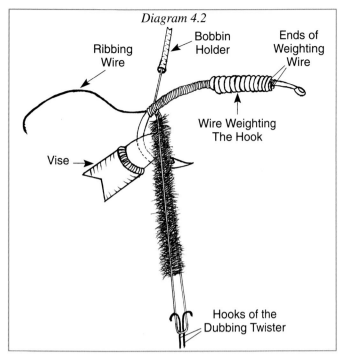

Diagram 4.2

Ribbing Wire

Bobbin Holder

Ends of Weighting Wire

Wire Weighting The Hook

Vise

Hooks of the Dubbing Twister

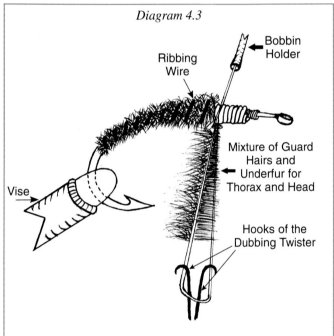

Diagram 4.3

Bobbin Holder

Ribbing Wire

Mixture of Guard Hairs and Underfur for Thorax and Head

Vise

Hooks of the Dubbing Twister

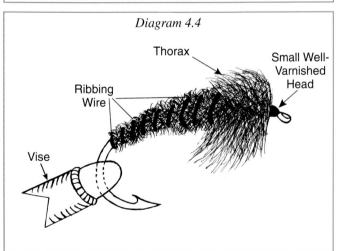

Diagram 4.4

Thorax

Small Well-Varnished Head

Ribbing Wire

Vise

Tying the Hairy Cream Larva

Step 1: Place the hook in the vise's jaws so that over half the bend is exposed.

Step 2: Wind the thread back along the shank to halfway around the bend then forward to a point 3/4 of the shank's length from the eye.

Step 3: Weight the hook using the Keel method.

Step 4: Wind the thread back to halfway around the bend; tie in the ribbing wire, form a dubbing loop and wind the thread forward to 1/4 of the shank's length from the eye. (Diagram 4.2) When determining the length of thread needed to form a dubbing loop for brushes and "Hair Hackles". Refer back to Chapter 2; point 2; Advantages of "Hair Hackles".

Step 5: To form the body, construct a very short-fibred dubbing brush of cream fur and wind it forward to 1/4 of the shank's length from the eye. (Diagram 4.3)

Step 6: Rib the body with seven spirals of gold wire, tie off and form a dubbing loop.

Step 7: Using fibres twice the length of those used for the body, form a dubbing brush of fiery brown fur or black Angel Hair. Wrap this brush forward to 1/2 an eye's length from the eye. Tie off. (Diagram 4.4)

Step 8: Form a small head, whip finish and varnish.

Hackle flies are the spider patterns with which North country and Scottish anglers have caught large baskets of fish during the past hundred years or so. In North America they are called soft-hackle flies.

Most fishermen now hold that they look like nymphs in the water, hence their effectiveness and popularity.

In order to introduce you to tying the "hair hackle" a simple spider pattern will be used to illustrate the process. Hair fibres are substituted for the feather fronds.

Refer back to Diagrams 3.3 to 3.10 in Chapter 3, which cover the construction of the hair hackle in detail. A "hair hackle" can be placed at any point on the hook's shank or

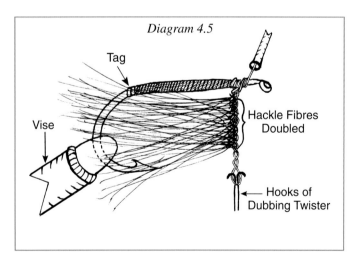

Diagram 4.5

Tag

Hackle Fibres Doubled

Vise

Hooks of Dubbing Twister

palmered along it. If the original dressing of a fly calls for a tail of feather fibres, a sparse "hair hackle" can be substituted for them thus adding life to the pattern.

❧ Hairy Black Spider ❧

Hook: TMC 3769, Partridge K4A, Daiichi 1530 sizes 10-16.

Thread: Black 6/0 or 8/0.

Tag: Flat silver tinsel.

Body: Black tying thread or floss silk.

Hackle: Natural or dyed black squirrel tail or any other fine black hair or fur.

Tying the Hairy Black Spider

Step 1: Place the hook in the vise's jaws.

Step 2: Starting an eye's length from the eye, wind the tying thread back to the hook's bend.

Step 3: Tie in the flat silver tinsel and wrap 2 turns of it for the tag.

Step 4: Form a slim body of tying thread or black floss finishing 2 eye lengths from the eye. (Diagram 4.5)

Step 5: Construct a "hair hackle" with fibre length 1 1/4 the hook's overall length. Make 2 tight turns of this hackle, one in front of the other, tie in and put 2 turns of thread over its base to slope the fibres slightly back. (Diagram 4.6)

Step 6: Form a small head, whip finish and varnish.

By combining dubbing brushes and "hair hackles," a wide variety of flies can be dressed. The first of these is a pupa pattern which can also be classified as a nymph.

❧ Hairy Olive Caddis Pupa ❧

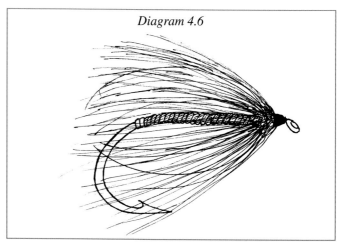

Hook: TMC 200R, Mustad 80050BR, or Daiichi 1270 sizes 8-16 wtd.

Thread: Yellow, olive or black 6/0 or 8/0.

Weight: Copper or lead wire.

Ribbing: Copper wire.

Body: Medium olive fur dubbing.

Thorax: Dark olive squirrel or rabbit fur.

Hackle: Dyed olive squirrel tail or dyed olive woodchuck guard hairs.

Head: Black fur or Angel Hair dubbing.

Tying the Hairy Olive Caddis Pupa

Step 1: Place the hook in the vise's jaws. Make sure the bend is exposed.

Step 2: Wind the tying thread back from 1/4 of the shank's length from the eye to halfway around the bend and forward to a point 3/4 of the shank's length from the eye.

Step 3: Using the Keel method, weight the hook.

Step 4: Return the tying thread to the point halfway around the bend of the hook and tie in the ribbing wire. Form a dubbing loop and wind the thread forward to a point 1/3 of the shank's length from the eye.

Step 5: Construct a short-haired dubbing brush of medium olive fur and wrap it forward to form the abdomen, finishing where the tying thread was left. Tie it off.

Step 6: Rib the abdomen with 7 spirals of wire and tie off. (Diagram 4.7)

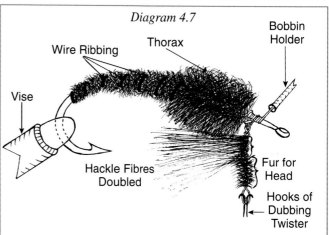

Diagram 4.6

Diagram 4.7

Wire Ribbing

Thorax

Bobbin Holder

Vise

Hackle Fibres Doubled

Fur for Head

Hooks of Dubbing Twister

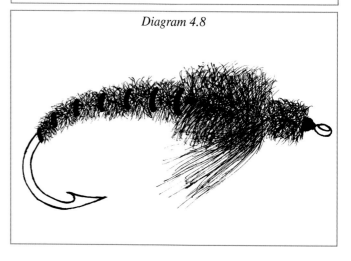

Diagram 4.8

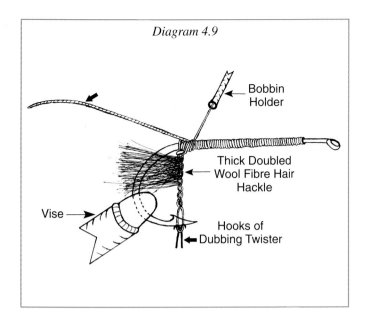

Diagram 4.9

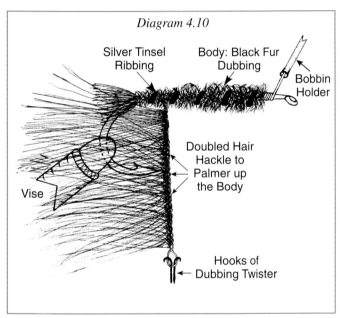

Diagram 4.10

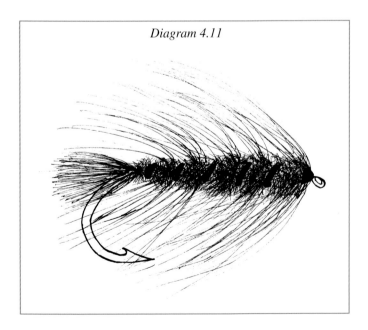

Diagram 4.11

Step 7: Construct a dubbing brush of dark olive fur with fibre length twice that of the abdomen's fur and wind it forward to form the thorax. Tie in the brush 2 eye lengths from the eye.

Step 8: Form another dubbing loop and first insert into it olive hair fibres equal in length to 1/2 the shank for the "hair hackle". Next insert into the same loop, short black fur fibres for the head. Spin the dubbing twister to form a "hair hackle" and a short dubbing brush for the head of the pupa. Carefully wrap this combination forward, stopping 1/2 an eye's length from the eye. Tie off. (Diagram 4.8).

Step 9: From a small head, whip finish and varnish.

Palmers like spider patterns have been around for a very long time. They and their many derivatives continue to be the best stand-bys for trout fishermen the world over. Again the "hair hackles" add life to an already great family of flies. A palmer universally known is the Zulu, so what better pattern is there to illustrate a palmer made with hair hackles.

⋙ The Hairy Zulu ⋘

Hook: TMC 3769, Partridge L2A, Mustad 3906B sizes 8-16.
Thread: Black 6/0 or 8/0.
Tail: Red wool fibres.
Ribbing: Flat silver tinsel.
Body: Black fur dubbing
Body hackle: Black hair palmered from second turn of tinsel.
Head hackle: Black hair 2 turns, more if fly is to be bushy.

Tying the Hairy Zulu

Step 1: Place the hook in the vise's jaws.

Step 2: Wind the tying thread from an eye's length from eye back to where the bend begins.

Step 3: Construct a "hair hackle" of red wool fibres equal to 1/2 shank's length. (They can always be trimmed if a short tail is required.) Wind 2 or 3 turns of this hackle to bulk up the tail. (Diagram 4.9)

Step 4: Tie in the flat silver tinsel ribbing and form a dubbing loop for the dubbed body. Wind thread forward to a point on the shank above the hook's point and form another dubbing loop for the palmer hackle. Continue the thread forward to 2 eye lengths from the eye.

Step 5: Construct a dubbing brush of short-fibred black fur and wrap it forward, finishing 2 eye's lengths from the eye. Tie in the brush. (Diagram 4.10)

Step 6: Rib the body with 5 turns of silver tinsel and tie off. Be careful to leave the second dubbing loop free. Prick out the dubbing using a gun-cleaning wire brush.

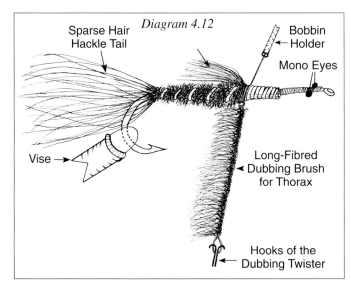

Diagram 4.12

Sparse Hair Hackle Tail

Bobbin Holder

Mono Eyes

Vise

Long-Fibred Dubbing Brush for Thorax

Hooks of the Dubbing Twister

Step 7: Form a "hair hackle" of black hair fibres equal in length to the overall length of the hook. Be sure that the hackle is long enough to palmer along the body and make 2 turns of hackle at the head of the fly. Palmer the "hair hackle" between the rib spirals, making a further 2 turns behind the eye and tie off. (Diagram 4.11)

Step 8: Form a small head, whip finish and varnish.

I mentioned the derivatives of the original palmer flies, these are many and varied. In the U.S.A., the famous Woolly Worm, followed by the now equally good Woolly Bugger. In Ireland, the Bumbles. In Scotland, the Ordies, my Trout Bombers and more recently my Bumpadabs. All the foregoing can be tied as Hairys by substituting hair or fur for feathers and body materials. In the Woolly Worm the tail of wool or cock hackle fibres is replaced by a wool or guard hairs "hair hackle". The body of chenille can remain or be replaced by a dubbing brush. For the palmered cock hackle, a "hair hackle" of grey fox tail is substituted. Where marabou is called for, arctic fox, opossum or raccoon fur can be used. As in the tail of the Woolly Bugger.

Now it is back to subsurface aquatic life and to the dressing of "Hairy" nymphs. One of the most widely

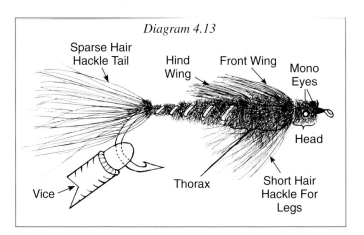

Diagram 4.13

Sparse Hair Hackle Tail

Hind Wing

Front Wing

Mono Eyes

Head

Thorax

Vise

Short Hair Hackle For Legs

distributed insects in the world is the damselfly. Fly-tyers in every continent have dressed representations of its nymph, as there is no doubt it is a major food of trout and many other fish. So the best example of dressing a "Hairy" nymph will be a damsel nymph.

❧ Hairy Olive Damsel Nymph (Red Eyed) ❧

Hook: TMC 5263, Mustad 9672, Partridge H1A, Daiichi 1720 sizes 8-14 wtd.

Thread: Yellow, olive or black 6/0 or 8/0.

Weight: Lead or copper wire.

Eyes: Red mono nymph eyes.

Tail: Dyed olive arctic fox or opossum fur.

Ribbing: Olive tinsel thread.

Body: Olive rabbit fur dubbing.

Hind wing: A small bunch of olive fur with guard hairs left in.

Thorax: Long fibred brush of olive fur with guard hairs left in.

Front wing: Dark grey opossum fur.

Hackle: Dyed olive squirrel tail

Head: Dark brown or black dubbing.

Tying the Hairy Olive Damsel Nymph (Red Eyed)

Step 1: Place the hook in the vise's jaws.

Step 2: Starting an eye's length from the eye, wind the thread back to the bend and forward to 3/4 of the shank's length from the eye.

Step 3: Weight the hook by the Keel method using lead wire.

Step 4: An eye's length from the eye tie in a pair of red painted mono nymph eyes on top of the shank. Use figure of eight bindings to secure the eyes.

Step 5: Run the thread back to the start of the hook's bend and construct an olive "hair hackle". The length of the hackle fibres should be equal to the length of the hook shank. To form the tail, make 2 turns of this hackle and tie off. (Diagram 4.12)

Step 6: Tie in the ribbing material and construct a dubbing of short-fibred olive fur. Wrap the dubbing brush forward to 1/3 of the shank's length from the eye. Tie off.

Step 7: Rib the body with 5 spirals of ribbing material. Tie off.

Step 8: Tie in the bunch of grey fur making sure that the wing is tent shaped over the body, and its fibres extend back to half the length of the abdomen. To achieve a secure tent-shaped wing make 2 tight turns of thread over the wing fibres, lift the butts of the wing material and wrap 2 more turns of thread under them tight up against the first 2 turns. Now make 2 turns over the fibres in front of the locking

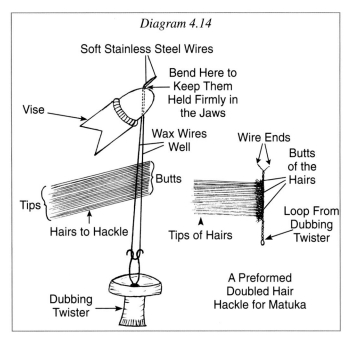

Diagram 4.14

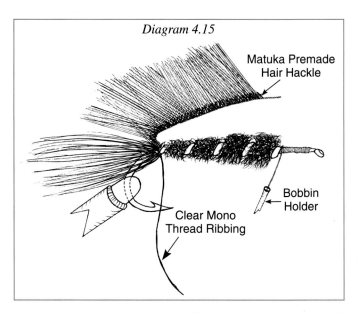

Diagram 4.15

bindings to spread the fibres around the top half of the body use a fingernail to push them halfway down each side of the body.

Step 9: Construct a dubbing brush of olive fur and guard hairs. Wind the thread forward over the wing butts to within 2 eye lengths from the eye. Trim off butt ends. Wrap the dubbing brush forward to form the thorax and tie off. Prick out the dubbing of the thorax.

Step 10: Tie in another tent-shaped wing. Cut off the butt ends of the wing and tie off just in front of the eyes. Return the thread to the base of the front wing. (Diagram 4.13)

Step 11: Construct a "hair hackle" of squirrel tail hair with fibre length equal to 1/2 the shank's length. Make 2 turns of this hackle and tie off.

Step 12: Form a head made of dubbing making certain that the dubbing is wrapped around the eyes in a figure of eight fashion.

Step 13: Tie off, whip finish and varnish.

In recent years, brass, copper, gold and silver beads have been incorporated as heads into dressings of pupae, larvae, nymphs and other patterns. They add weight to the front of flies, and there is little doubt that the jigging action imparted enhances the effectiveness of many patterns. Any Hairy pattern can be changed into a Beaded Hairy by simply slipping a bead onto a hook and fixing it behind the eye before dressing the rest of the fly. One of the most important "hair hackles" used in the Hairys is the preformed one. It is incorporated into the dressings of Matukas, sedges, fry and shrimp patterns. It is simple to make as it is merely a dubbing brush with long hair. The only difficulties I have found are when hairs cross over each other and are not spread out evenly in the dubbing loop. If you eliminate these problems, fibres of almost any length can be formed into a "hair hackle".

Tying the preformed "hair hackle"

Step 1: Cut a length of very fine soft stainless steel wire equal to twice the length of the required dubbing loop.

Step 2: Place the 2 ends of the wire in the vise's jaws. Bend the ends of the wire over to prevent them slipping out. (Diagram 4.14)

Step 3: Wax the wire, insert the amount of fibres required for the "hair hackle", trim the butts of the fibres to 1/16 or 1/8 of an inch, spin the twister and form the hackle. Refer back to Chapter 3 if you are uncertain about the process.

Step 4: Make sure that the fibres are firmly held by the twisted wire. Double the hackle, remove the twister and there you have a dubbing brush hackle ready for use.

There are two main uses for preformed "hair hackles". Firstly for Matuka-style flies and secondly as a palmer hackle. Dressing of a Hairy Olive Matuka will illustrate the dressing of all hair Matukas.

❧ Hairy Olive Matuka ❧

Hook: TMC 5263, Daiichi 1720 or 2220, Mustad 9672 or 79580 sizes 4-12.

Thread: Black or olive 6/0.

Tag: Oval gold tinsel.

Tail: Dyed olive squirrel tail.

Ribbings: Oval gold tinsel and to hold Matuka hackle, clear nylon thread.

Body: First 3/4 of the body olive dubbing. Last 1/4 red dubbing.

Matuka hackle: Preformed "hair hackle" of dyed olive squirrel.

Head hackle: Hair hackle of dyed olive squirrel.

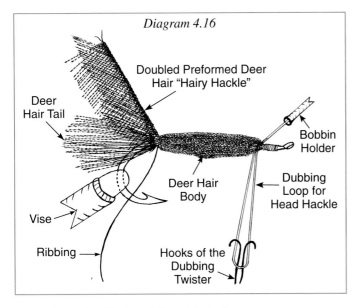

Diagram 4.16

Deer Hair Tail

Doubled Preformed Deer Hair "Hairy Hackle"

Bobbin Holder

Vise

Deer Hair Body

Dubbing Loop for Head Hackle

Ribbing

Hooks of the Dubbing Twister

Tying the Hairy Olive Matuka (Diagram 4.15)

Step 1: Place hook in vise's jaws.

Step 2: Starting 2 eye lengths from the eye, wind the thread back to the bend.

Step 3: Tie in oval gold tinsel and form the tag. The tag should stretch from the barb to hook's point on the shank.

Step 4: Construct a "hair hackle" of dyed olive squirrel tail. Hair length equal to shank's length. Make 2 turns of this hackle and tie off.

Step 5: Tie in the ribbing materials and preformed "hair hackle" whose fibre lengths should be equal to 1/2 shank's length. Tie off making sure the wire of the hackle lies along the top of the shank, and its fibres are over the tail.

Step 6: Construct a dubbing brush of olive fur. Wrap this brush forward over 3/4 of shank. Tie off. Construct another dubbing brush of red fur and wind it forward to 2 1/2 eye lengths from the eye. Tie off.

Step 7: Rib body with gold oval tinsel. Bend the Matuka hackle over the back of the body and rib with 5 spirals of nylon thread through the fibres of the Matuka hackle. Tie off the hackle and nylon ribbing.

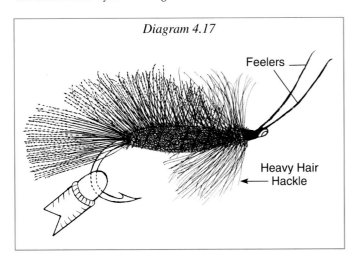

Diagram 4.17

Feelers

Heavy Hair Hackle

Step 8: Construct a "hair hackle" of olive squirrel tail, wind it forward and tie off an eye's length from the eye.

Step 9: Form a head, whip finish and varnish.

Something new next: Matuka dry flies, namely sedges, made mainly from deer hair to give them better floating properties.

◈ **Hairy Green Sedge** ◈

Hook: Partridge 01 Wilson Single Salmon sizes 10-16, or TMC 5212 sizes 4-10.

Thread: Green or black 6/0 or 8/0.

Tail: A bunch of natural deer hair.

Ribbing: Clear nylon thread.

Wing: Preformed "hair hackle" of natural deer hair.

Body: A dubbing brush made of dyed-green deer hair.

Hackle: Ginger hair.

Antennae: Dark moose mane, 2 strands.

Tying the Hairy Green Sedge

Step 1: Place hook in vise's jaws.

Step 2: Starting 2 eye's lengths from the eye wind the thread back to bend.

Step 3: Tie in a thick bunch of deer hair, the points extending 1/2 shank's length out from bend, and the butts tied on top of the shank to 1/4 of shank's length from the eye. This helps the fly to float. (Diagram 4.16)

Step 4: Tie in ribbing and the preformed Matuka hackle. The length of fibres in this hackle equal to 1/2 shank's length.

Step 5: Form a dubbing brush of short-fibred green deer hair. Wrap it forward to 1/4 of shank's length from the eye. Tie off and trim the body, flat beneath the shank, sloping at an angle upwards towards the tail and angled outwards at the sides from head to tail.

Step 6: Bring Matuka hackle forward over the top of the body. It should bite into the hair on top of the body. Tie off.

Step 7: Spiral the ribbing forward in tight turns to hold Matuka hackle in place on top of the body.

Step 8: Construct a ginger "hair hackle" with fibre length equal to width of hook's gape. Wind hackle forward to 1 eye length from eye, and tie off. (Diagram 4.17)

Step 9: Tie in the antennae just behind the eye.

Step 10: Form a head, whip finish and varnish.

The preformed "hair hackle" used for palmering has several advantages. The wire base can replace ribbing, as in my Hairy Trout Bombers and Bumpadabs. When tying a batch of flies, hackles with the same fibre lengths can be preformed thus cutting down the tying time. Several hackles of equal width can be formed in a single dubbing loop.

There is one material that has been rather glossed over and that is deer hair; my favourite working medium. I prefer to spin and or stack deer-hair when forming Muddler heads and the bodies of bugs. Nevertheless as seen from dressing the Hairy sedge patterns, preformed deer-hair brushes and hackles together with preformed palmer hackles are very useful. Preformed deer hair brushes and palmer hackles can be used in dressing Hairy Trout Bombers.

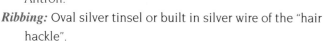

⊰⊱ Clan Chief Hairy Trout Bomber ⊰⊱

Hook: Partridge YL2A,
    Sprite International,
    sizes 8-14, TMC 102Y
    sizes 9-15.
Thread: Black 6/0 or 8/0.
Tag: Flat silver tinsel.
Tail: Red over yellow
    Antron.
Ribbing: Oval silver tinsel or built in silver wire of the "hair hackle".
Body: Black deer-hair dubbing brush.
Hackle: Mixed black and red haired preformed "hair hackle".
Head hackle: Black hair.

Tying the Clan Chief Hairy Trout Bomber

Step 1: Place hook in vise's jaws.
Step 2: Form a firm thread base on the shank from 2 eye lengths from eye to above the hook point.
Step 3: Tie in flat silver tinsel and form a tag with it stretching from above the barb to above the point of the hook.
Step 4: Construct a 2-sectioned "hair hackle". First section nearest the hook, yellow Antron fibres. Second section up against the first, red Antron fibres. Wind this hackle around the shank above the point. Trim to length just beyond bend of hook.
Step 5: Tie in the mixed red and black fibred preformed "hair hackle" along the underside of the hook shank.
Step 6: Form a dubbing brush of short-fibred black deer hair. Wrap this dubbing brush forward to 2 eye lengths from the eye and tie in.
Step 7: Palmer 5 spirals of the hackle forward over the body and tie in.
Step 8: Form a black fibred "hair hackle", make 2 turns and tie in.
Step 9: Form a small head, whip finish and varnish.

Just as any of the Hairys can be turned into a gold head by adding a bead before dressing the rest of the fly, so Hairy Muddlers can be tied by leaving the front 1/4 of the shank bare for the Muddler's head and dressing the rest of the fly first. The head can be formed using a combined deer-hair hackle and dubbing brush similar to the combination used for the hackle and head of the Hairy Caddis Pupa.

The basic techniques for dressing the Hairys have now been covered so on to some refinements that can be made to "hair hackles".
1. With a little modification, a long-fibred "hair hackle" of Antron wool at the hook's bend can represent a shuck on a stillborn dun or an imago as it escapes from its nymphal skin. Representations of emergent mayflies and midges best illustrate this use of "hair hackles" in forming shucks.

⊰⊱ Hairy Olive Mayfly Emerger ⊰⊱

Hook: TMC 5212,
    Partridge H1A,
    Mustad 94831, Daiichi
    1280 sizes 10-16.
Thread: Yellow or olive 6/0
    or 8/0.
Shuck: Olive or medium
    olive Antron wool fibres.
Tail: Medium olive wood chuck guard hairs.
Ribbing: Olive around tinsel.
Body: Medium olive dubbing.
Wings: Small bunches of pale olive deer hair on either side of the body.
Thorax: Olive dubbing.
Hackle: Medium olive woodchuck guard hairs.
Method
Step 1: Place hook in vise's jaws with bend exposed.
Step 2: Wind thread from 2 eye lengths from the eye back to bend of hook.
Step 3: Construct a sparse "hair hackle" of Antron wool with fibre length equal to shank's length. Wrap 1 turn of this hackle, tie in and half hitch. Stroke the fibres back making sure that they are evenly distributed around the shank. Hold the tips together with a pair of hackle pliers and make 3 half hitches on top of one another 1/8 of an inch from the fibre tips. Put a drop of super glue on the half hitches to hold them in place.
Step 4: Construct a very sparse "hair hackle" of woodchuck guard hairs dyed olive, with fibre length equal to 1/2 the shank. Make 1 turn of this hackle close up against the shuck. Tie off and half hitch.

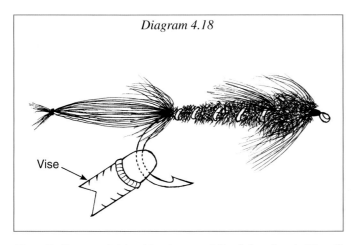

Diagram 4.18

Vise

Step 5: Form a dubbed body over 2/3 of the shank. Tie off and spiral 5 turns of ribbing.

Step 6: Tie in the 2 bunches of deer hair on either side of the body to form emergent wings. The length of the wings should equal 1/2 shank length. (Diagram 4.18)

Step 7: Form a dubbed thorax to within 1 1/2 eye lengths from the eye. Tie off.

Step 8: Construct a "hair hackle" with fibre length equal to the hook's gape and wide enough to make 2 turns around the shank. Wrap 2 turns of hackle and tie off.

Step 9: Form a small head, whip finish.

❧ Hairy Black Midge Emerger ❧

Hook: Partridge YK2B, TMC
    2487, daiichi 1150, sizes 10-16.
Thread: Black 6/0 or 8/0.
Shuck tail: Grey Antron wool.
Tail: White Antron wool.
Ribbing: Silver wire.
Body: Black dubbing (thin).
Wing buds: Olive over orange Antron wool.
Thorax: Black dubbing.
Hackle: Black squirrel tail.
Gills: White Antron wool.

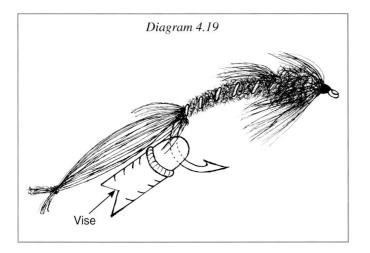

Diagram 4.19

Vise

Tying the Hairy Black Midge Emerger (Diagrams 4.19)

Step 1: Place the hook in the vise's jaws.

Step 2: Form a firm thread base along the shank of the hook.

Step 3: At the hook's bend construct a sparse "hair hackle" of Antron wool with fibre length equal to the shank's length. Wrap 1 turn of this hackle, tie in and half hitch. Stroke the fibres making sure that they are evenly distributed around the shank. Hold the tips of the hackle together with a pair of hackle pliers and make 3 half hitches on top of one another 1/8 of an inch from the fibre tips. Put a drop of super glue on the half hitches to hold them in place.

Step 4: Construct a very short-fibred "hair hackle" of white Antron wool and wrap 2 turns of it close up against the shuck. Tie off and half hitch.

Step 5: Form a very thin dubbed body over 2/3 of the shank. Tie off and spiral 5 turns of ribbing and again tie off.

Step 6: Tie in short wing buds of olive over orange Antron wool.

Step 7: Form a thorax of black dubbing, stopping 2 eye lengths from the eye.

Step 8: Make 2 turns of a "hair hackle" of black squirrel tail and tie it in.

Step 9: Form a short-fibred dubbing brush of white Antron wool and make 2 turns of it in front of the hackle and tie off.

Step 10: Form a small head, whip finish and varnish.

And now for the last two and most challenging patterns. The first being Hairy freshwater shrimps.

❧ Hairy Olive Shrimp ❧

Hook: Partridge YK2B,
    Daiichi 1150, sizes 10-16 wtd.
Thread: Yellow or olive
    6/0 or 8/0.
Weight: Copper or lead wire.
Antennae: 2 strands of
    pearl Crystal Hair.
Tail Hackle: Short fibred
    olive woodchuck fur.
Eyes: Nylon mono nymph eyes painted black.
Legs: Preformed hackle of olive woodchuck underfur.
Ribbing: Clear nylon thread.
Body: Pale olive dubbing.
Shellback: Olive grey squirrel tail

Tying the Hairy Olive Shrimp

Step 1: Place the hook in the vise's jaws with the bend well exposed.

 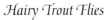

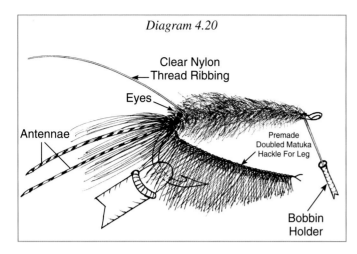

Diagram 4.20

Clear Nylon
Thread Ribbing

Eyes

Antennae

Premade
Doubled Matuka
Hackle For Leg

Bobbin
Holder

Step 2: Form a firm thread base from 1 eye length from the eye to halfway around the hook's bend.

Step 3: Using the keel method, weight the hook over the rear 3/4 of the shank. As shrimp swim on their backs, upright or on their sides, the keel can be placed on the top, underneath or along the sides of the hook's shank. An interesting wobbling, spoon-like action is imparted into the fly if the keel is placed along one side or the other and it is attached to the leader with a Duncan loop knot.

Step 4: Tie in 2 strands of crystal hair for the antennae. Their length equal to 1 1/4 times the shank's length. (Diagram 4.20)

Step 5: Construct a short-fibred sparse, "hair hackle" of woodchuck guard hairs with a small quantity of underfur left in. The guard hairs should be 1/2 the length of the antennae and underfur 1/4 of their length. Make 2 turns of the hackle and tie off.

Step 6: Using figure-of-eight bindings, tie in a pair of black painted mono nymph eyes close up against the tail hackle and tie off.

Step 7: Tie in the ribbing and, under the shank, the pre-formed leg's hackle. The fibre length on this hackle should be equal to the hook's gape.

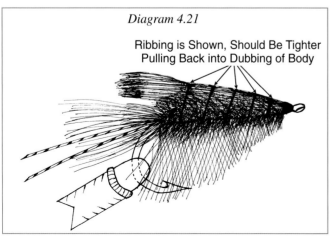

Diagram 4.21

Ribbing is Shown, Should Be Tighter
Pulling Back into Dubbing of Body

Step 8: Form a dubbing brush for the body and wrap it forward to 1 1/2 eye lengths from the eye and tie in.

Step 9: Bring the leg's hackle forward, tie in 1 1/2 eye lengths from the eye.

Step 10: Tie in a tent-shaped wing for the shell back. The tips of the wing fibres should protrude just beyond the bend of the hook.

Step 11: Rib the fly, pulling the ribbing spirals tight into leg's hackle and the shell back to form the body segments. Tie in the ribbing. (Diagram 4.21)

Step 12: Form a small head, whip finish and varnish.

And now for the Hairy Fry or Hairy Baitfish flies that incorporate most of the foregoing techniques and include deer hair or spun wool heads. They can be tied on low water salmon hooks, keel hooks or bent-shank nymph hooks; the latter two styles making the flies weedless.

❧ Hairy Fry or Baitfish ❧
❧ Hairy Minnow ❧

Hook: Partridge N, TMC 7989, Daiichi 2421 sizes 4-12 wtd.

Weedless hook: Keel hook or Daiichi 1730 sizes 4-12 wtd.

Thread: Green or tan 6/0 or 8/0.

Weight: Lead or tungsten wire.

Tail: Black-tipped woodchuck guard hairs.

Ribbing: Clear nylon.

Back: Premade Matuka "hair hackle" of dyed olive rabbit fur.

Body: Mixture of olive and cream fur dubbing.
Pectoral fins: Black-tipped woodchuck guard hairs.

Gills: Dyed-red fur dubbing.

Collar: White deer hair below the shank. Olive deer hair on top of the shank.

Head: Olive stacked over creamy grey deer hair trimmed to shape.

Eyes: Brown or yellow epoxy eyes.

Tying the Hairy Minnow

Step 1: Place the hook in the vise's jaws.

Step 2: Form a firm thread base stretching from 1/3 of the shank's length from the eye to the hook's bend.

Step 3: Weight the hook by using the keel method.

Step 4: Construct a "hair hackle" of black-tipped woodchuck guard hairs with fibre length equal to 1/2 shank's length. The width of the hackle should be wide enough to

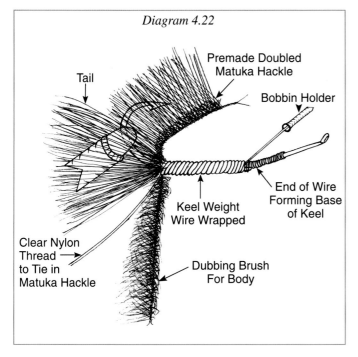

Diagram 4.22

Tail

Premade Doubled Matuka Hackle

Bobbin Holder

End of Wire Forming Base of Keel

Keel Weight Wire Wrapped

Clear Nylon Thread to Tie in Matuka Hackle

Dubbing Brush For Body

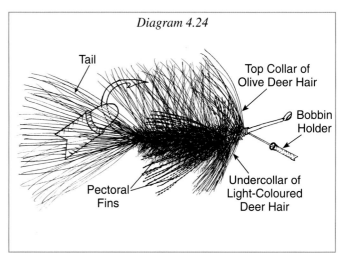

Diagram 4.24

Tail

Top Collar of Olive Deer Hair

Bobbin Holder

Pectoral Fins

Undercollar of Light-Coloured Deer Hair

make 2 turns around the shank. Wind 2 tight turns of the hackle, and tie off.

Step 5: Tie in ribbing and Matuka hackle. (Diagram 4.22)

Step 6: Form a dubbing brush of a 50/50 mixture of cream and olive fur and wind it forward to 1/3 of the shank's length from the eye. Tie off, and make 2 half hitches. (Diagram 4.22)

Step 7: Bring the premade Matuka hackle over the back of the body and tie in.

Step 8: Rib the body with 5 spirals of thread, making certain that the ribbing is tight and no fibres of the Matuka hackle are tied in.

Step 9: Construct a "hair hackle" of black-tipped woodchuck guard hairs and wrap 2 turns of it over the bindings holding body dubbing brush, Matuka hackle and ribbing. To form the

pectoral fins divide the hackle with figure of eight bindings so that equal amounts of fibres stick out on either side of the body. (Diagram 4.23)

Step 10: Form a dubbing brush of short-fibred red fur and figure-of-eight it around the pectoral fins. Tie in and half hitch. (Diagram 4.24)

Step 11: On the underside of the body, tie in a bunch of creamy grey deer hair, adjust so that it surrounds 1/2 the hook shank. On the top side of the hook shank, tie in a bunch of olive deer hair and adjust it to meet the creamy grey hair. (Diagram 4.24)

Step 12: Stack olive over creamy grey deer hair to form the head of the fry. Trim the head, flat on the sides and arounded top and bottom. Final shaping should be done with a razor blade. (Diagram 4.25)

Step 13: Burn hollows into the sides of the head and attach eyes in them with waterproof glue.

Step 14: Form a small head, whip finish and varnish.

With the Hairy Minnow, the chapter on dressing of Hairy trout flies is completed and further refinements to "hair hackles" will be left to the chapters on sea flies and bass bugs.

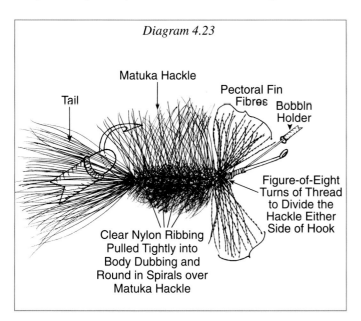

Diagram 4.23

Tail

Matuka Hackle

Pectoral Fin Fibres

Bobbin Holder

Figure-of-Eight Turns of Thread to Divide the Hackle Either Side of Hook

Clear Nylon Ribbing Pulled Tightly into Body Dubbing and Round in Spirals over Matuka Hackle

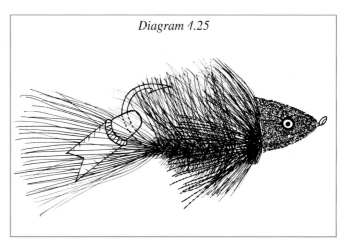

Diagram 4.25

Chapter 5

Salmon, Sea Trout & Steelhead Flies

Freshwater fly fishermen consider the Atlantic salmon and its relative, the Pacific salmon as kings of the rivers and lakes, and as such, a formidable prey. However they are not the only migratory occupants of these waters. They share them with sea trout in Europe and steelhead in North America. Both steelhead and sea trout are equally fine fighters, but easier to catch than salmon.

In the 19th century, a myth arose among anglers that because the salmon was a king of fish it would choose to eat only those creatures that were beautiful to look at, and what could be more beautiful than a butterfly. Thus the wings of salmon flies were built in glorious patterns using brightly coloured strips of feathers. They caught fish and the art of tying full-dress salmon flies was born.

In truth, salmon rarely feed on anything when returning from the sea to their birthplace in the headwaters of rivers. There are several theories as to why they should feed at all in fresh water after gorging themselves on the rich food of the seas and oceans. The first one is that instinctively they are reminded of their youth when, as parr, they fed on insects and other freshwater aquatic life. Secondly, they take representations of prawns, shrimps and sand eels as they fed on these in the sea, and just as people get a craving now and again for certain types of food, so do they. Lastly, they have a killer instinct and get annoyed at a procession of flies and lures being pulled past them. The only way they can get rid of these irritants is to bite them and so they get caught.

Sea trout and steelhead do feed in fresh water, and at times voraciously so, taking mice, crayfish, fry and a variety of insects, so representations of these must be tied. On the other hand, at times they seem to be timid feeders and come short to flies, nipping at their tails. In order to counteract this irritating trait many sea trout and steelhead flies are tied with no tail and in the style of low-water salmon flies. In Britain trailer hooks are often added which have partially succeeded in overcoming the problem. Enough about the feeding habits of these fish and on to the Hairys that have enticed them to rise.

It is a fact that traditionally the catalogues of tackle dealers list flies under the species of fish they are designed to catch. In Britain they are listed under trout, sea trout, salmon and more recently under sea and pike flies as well. In the U.S.A. the number of species of fish that are caught by fly-rodders is far greater, so there are many more categories under which flies may be listed. I mention this because various species of fish don't seem to classify flies in the same way as we do. Salmon, steelhead, sea trout and trout are quite willing to rise to flies that are specifically listed for the other species.

While fishing for salmon, I have caught sea trout and brown trout on salmon flies, and my father quite regularly rose and occasionally landed a salmon when fishing for trout. In this chapter, I am classifying flies under style rather than under the species of fish they are supposed to catch. However in the patterns section they will be listed under species.

Nowadays very few simple hackle or palmer flies are fished for salmon, steelhead or sea trout. However my Leggys, Hairy salmon flies and Bumpadabs (the name for, and the dressings of, these flies are derived from Irish bumbles and dabblers and old-fashioned palmers) are catching salmon and sea trout in Ireland and Scotland. There is no reason why they should not catch steelhead and Pacific salmon in the rivers of western North America. Leggys are palmer flies with extra-long sparse head hackles and are easy to tie.

⋙ Hairy Golden Olive Leggy ⋘

Hook: Singles: Partridge YL2A sizes 8-14. Doubles: Partridge R2A sizes 10-16.
Thread: Yellow 6/0 or 8/0.
Tag: Flat gold tinsel.
Tail: Golden olive hair.
Ribbing: Gold oval or wire.
Palmer hackle: Preformed ginger hair, Spey style.
Body: Golden olive fur dubbing.
Head hackle No. 1: Fine golden olive bucktail.
Head hackle No. 2: Blue jay.
<u>Note:</u> If you wish single, double and treble salmon hooks can be substituted for the trout hooks.

Tying the Hairy Golden Olive Leggy

Step 1: Place the hook in the vise's jaws.
Step 2: Form a firm thread foundation an eye's length from the eye to the hook's bend.
Step 3: Tie in the flat gold tinsel, form the tag and tie off.
Step 4: Construct a sparse "hair hackle" of golden olive hair with fibre length equal to the hook shank's length, wrap 1 turn and tie in.
Step 5: Tie in the ribbing and the preformed hackle. The fibre length in the hackle equal to 1 1/2 times the length of the hook's shank. (Diagram 5.0)

Step 6: Form a dubbed body which should finish 3 eye lengths from the eye, and tie off.

Step 7: Wind 5 spirals of the ribbing over the body, tie in and wind the palmer hackle between the ribbing spirals and tie it off.

Step 8: The 2 head hackles should be formed in one dubbing loop. Therefore it is important to judge the correct amount of bucktail and blue jay fibres required to make 1 complete turn of each hackle. Use the circumference formula to work this out. The length of fibres in the bucktail hackle must be equal to 2 hook shank's lengths. The blue jay fibres must be equal in length to 1 1/2 times the width of the hook's gape. Spin the dubbing twister and double the resultant hackle. Wrap it forward and tie in. (Diagram 5.1)

Step 9: Form a neat head, whip finish and varnish.

_____

Following on from the Leggys are my Bumpadabs in which I have combined Kingsmill Moore's famous Irish (bum)bles with traditional (pa)lmers and the relatively new Irish patterns, the (dab)blers. They can be fished anywhere on a cast, but usually on the top or middle dropper. Initially they were made for catching brown and sea trout, but salmon have been taken on the black, claret and golden-olive versions. Sea trout sometimes come short to these flies so a trailer hook can be added if you wish. When dressed on long-shank hooks, with the addition of a deer-hair collar and head, they can be turned into wake flies. The blue jay is replaced with a collar of dyed-blue deer hair. Several versions are listed in the patterns section of this book.

❧ **Hairy Claret Bumpadab** ❧

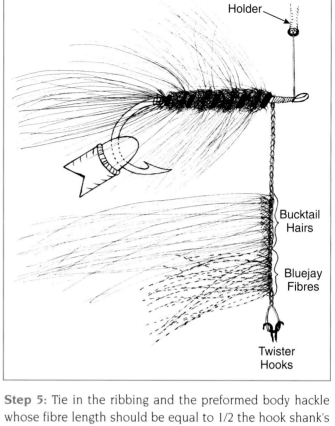
Diagram 5.0

Hook: Partridge YL2A,
    TMC 5210 sizes 6-12.
Thread: Red or black 6/0
    or 8/0.
Tag: Flat gold tinsel.
Tail: Dyed orange black-
    tipped woodchuck hair.
Ribbing: Oval gold tinsel.
Body hackle: Preformed of black hair.
Body: Claret fur dubbing.
Head hackle No. 1: Dyed claret grey squirrel tail hair.
Head hackle No. 2: Blue jay.

Tying the Hairy Claret Bumpadab
(Refer to Diagrams 5.0 and 5.1)

Step 1: Place the hook in the vise's jaws.

Step 2: Form a firm thread foundation 1 eye length from the eye to the hook's bend.

Step 3: Tie in the flat gold tinsel and form the tag, tie in and half hitch.

Step 4: Construct a sparse tail hackle with fibre length equal to the 3/4 of hook shank's length. Wrap it forward and tie it off.

Step 5: Tie in the ribbing and the preformed body hackle whose fibre length should be equal to 1/2 the hook shank's length.

Step 6: Form a claret fur dubbed body which should be tied off 3 eye lengths from the eye. Spiral 5 tight turns of the ribbing along the body and tie off.

Step 7: Palmer the body hackle forward between the ribbing, tie off and half hitch.

Step 8: Form a dubbing loop and insert into it the fibres of the 2 front hackles. Number 1 hackle should have fibre length equal to 1 1/2 times the shank's length, and number 2 hackle should have fibre length equal to 1 1/2 times the width of the hook's gape. As with the Leggys, one turn of

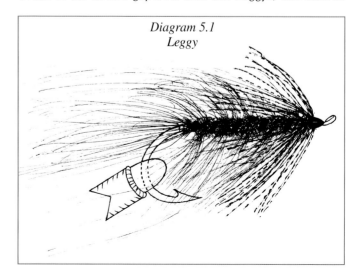
Diagram 5.1
Leggy

each hackle is required. Use the circumference formula to determine the widths of the two hackles. Spin the dubbing twister, double the hackles and wrap them forward finishing an eye's length from the eye, tie in.

Step 9: Form a neat head, whip finish and varnish.

Since the early 20th century, tandem lures have been used by fishermen to catch sea trout. As the name suggests, the tandem mount consists of a double or single front hook with one or two hooks mounted in line behind it. The fairly light dressing is usually confined to the front hook. It is not on the traditional tandem mount itself that I dress my patterns, but on one of its derivatives, the trailer mount. Under the influence of Hugh Falkus, Malcolm Greenhalgh and others, flies tied on this mount have become very popular and can prove successful under all water conditions and at all times of day and night. They are especially useful when fish are coming short. The mount is simple to construct and easy to dress. It consists of a single hook at the front with a small treble attached to nylon monofilament mounted at the bend of the front hook.

❧ Tandem Mount ❧
Hooks: Front single Partridge 01 sizes 4-12. Rear treble, Partridge X3BL sizes 8-16.
Connecting material: Monofilament nylon 10-pound to 20-pound test.
Thread: Black, red or yellow 6/0.

Tying the Tandem Mount
(Diagrams 5.2, 5.3 and 5.4)

Step 1: Place the treble hook in the vise's jaws and form a firm thread foundation on its shank.

Step 2: Take a 6- to 10-inch length of monofilament of the required breaking strain, pass one end of it through eye of the treble hook and around the bend of one of its hook prongs. Bring the end forward along the shank and through the hook's eye. Bind in the 2 strands of the nylon loop along the shank to the eye, tie off, whip finish, varnish and lay to one side. This is the end of the first stage of production. Try to use mass-production methods when making up these mounts as it saves time in the long run.

Step 3: Place the front hook in the vise's jaws and form a firm thread foundation ending at the bend of the hook. Pass the ends of the monofilament loop through the eye of the front hook, make sure the strands of the nylon lie on either side of the hook shank. Make 5 or 6 turns of thread around the nylon strands and the shank of the front hook. Adjust the distance between the rear hook and the front hook by pulling the nylon ends or the rear hook. I like the eye of the rear hook to be above the bend of the front hook. Wind the thread in tight touching turns to the eye of the front hook. Bend the ends of the nylon back over the shank of the front hook and through the eye of the treble. Bind the nylon strands together along the shank of the front hook and half hitch. Now place the rear hook in the vise's jaws and continue binding the thread in touching turns over the nylon

strands and shank of rear hook. Cut off the ends of the nylon, half hitch, whip finish and varnish the bindings of the whole mount. Leave it to dry thoroughly before dressing it.

There are two main uses to which the trailer mount can be put. Firstly, flies to hook fish coming short. Traditional sea-trout flies are tied on trailer mounts. However the Hairys with their pulsating action, tied on the same mounts, seem to attract and hook more fish. Therefore all "Hairy" Leggies, Bumpadabs and Spey type flies can be dressed on a tandem mount if you so wish.

In 1953 I invented the Gorbenmac (a winged wet fly) which in the following years caught many rainbow and brown trout from the rivers and streams of the Amatola mountains of South Africa. The original dressing appears on page 31.

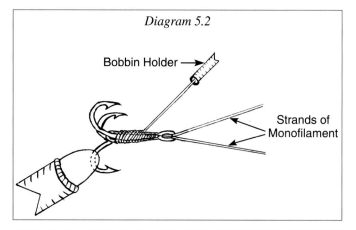

Diagram 5.2

Bobbin Holder →

Strands of Monofilament

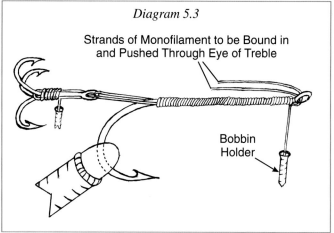

Diagram 5.3

Strands of Monofilament to be Bound in and Pushed Through Eye of Treble

Bobbin Holder

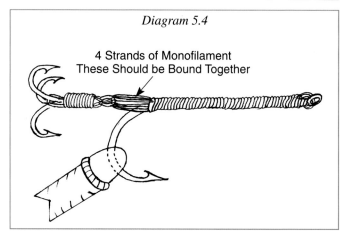

Diagram 5.4

4 Strands of Monofilament These Should be Bound Together

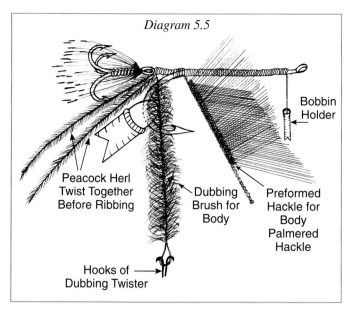

Diagram 5.5

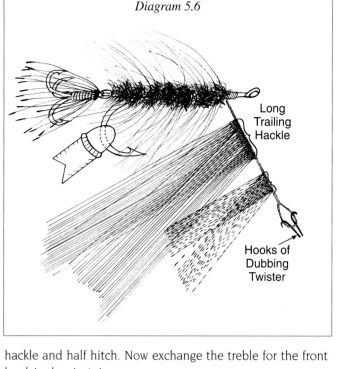

Diagram 5.6

Diagram 5.5 labels: Peacock Herl Twist Together Before Ribbing; Dubbing Brush for Body; Preformed Hackle for Body Palmered Hackle; Bobbin Holder; Hooks of Dubbing Twister

Diagram 5.6 labels: Long Trailing Hackle; Hooks of Dubbing Twister

Hook: Mustad 94840, sizes 6-12.

Thread: Black or red stout silk.

Tail: Golden pheasant tippet fibres.

Ribbing: Bronze peacock herl.

Body: Red seal's fur dubbing.

Hackle: Blue jay.

Wings: Sections of blue mallard wing feathers.

Recently I have changed the original dressing into one for a "Hairy" Bumpadab which has become a successful loch and sea trout fly. It can be dressed on single or double hooks or, as in the example given below, as a trailer tandem.

⋘ Hairy Gorbenmac Bumpadab ⋙

Hook: Trailer tandem mount.

Thread: Black or red 6/0.

Tag: Braided silver Mylar on treble hook.

Tail: Black tipped woodchuck hair dyed orange.

Ribbing: Dubbing brush of bronze peacock herl.

Body hackle: Preformed dyed red hair.

Body: Red fur dubbing.

Head hackle No. 1: Grey squirrel tail dyed dark blue.

Head hackle No. 2: Blue jay.

Tying the Hairy Gorbenmac Bumpadab
(Diagrams 5.5 and 5.6)

Step 1: Place treble hook in the vise's jaws.

Step 2: Tie in silver Mylar and wrap it forward to 1 eye length from the eye and tie in.

Step 3: Construct a sparse "hair hackle" of dyed orange black-tipped woodchuck hair, with fibre length equal to the overall length of the treble hook. Wind the hackle forward to the base of the eye, half hitch and whip finish.

Step 4: On the nylon connecting link just in front of the eye of the treble, tie in the ribbing brush and the preformed body

hackle and half hitch. Now exchange the treble for the front hook in the vise's jaws.

Step 5: Form a red fur dubbing brush at the eye of the treble. Wind the tying thread forward to 3 eye lengths from the eye of the front hook. Wrap the dubbing brush forward to the same point and tie in.

Step 6: Rib the body with 5 spirals of the peacock herl brush and tie in. Next palmer the body hackle forward between the ribbing spirals and tie in.

Step 7: Form a dubbing loop and insert into it the fibres of the 2 front head hackles. Number 1 hackle should have fibre length equal to the distance between the base of the eye of the front hook to the bends of the hooks on the treble. Number 2 hackle should have fibre length half the length of the front hook's shank. As with the Leggies and the other Bumpadabs only one turn of each hackle is required so check the widths of the bunches of fibres before spinning the dubbing twister and doubling the hackles. Wrap the hackles forward to an eye's length from the eye and tie in.

Step 8: Form a neat head, whip finish and varnish.

Secondly, a trailer mount can be used in the dressing of surface wake lures.

Surface wake flies tied on single hooks have been used for many years in the rivers of North America by steelhead fishermen. In Britain and Ireland it seems to take a very long time for fishermen to adopt the successful methods and well-tried techniques of their American cousins. The few sea-trout fishermen who have fished with surface wake flies and lures have had wonderfully exciting sport. They know now that these flies do catch quantities of sea trout and big ones at that. There is something about a surface fly or lure that seems to instill a killer instinct in all fish. I

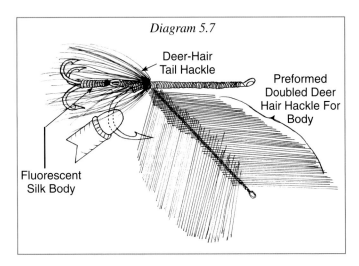

Diagram 5.7

Deer-Hair
Tail Hackle

Preformed
Doubled Deer
Hair Hackle For
Body

Fluorescent
Silk Body

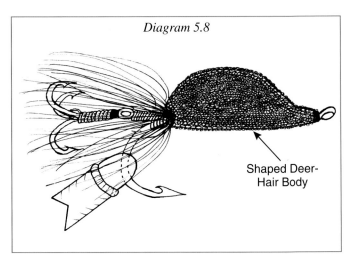

Diagram 5.8

Shaped Deer-
Hair Body

have found that fish caught on surface lures seem to put up a better fight than those taken on a subsurface fly. By simply adding a deer-hair body and/or head to any fly pattern you can create a surface wake fly. Bombers and Muddlers are examples of this. There are two types of deer-hair head used on wake flies: the pointed one of the slider which is a quiet lure producing a small wake, and the flat-faced one of the popper or chugger that produces a popping sound and/or a bubbling wide wake. In Britain there is one significant surface wake lure that is fished at night for sea trout, namely the Night Muddler. Tie this simple deer-hair bug on a trailer tandem and you will not be sorry with the results it produces. Why I have included this lure with the Hairys is because it can be tied with one preformed deer-hair hackle.

✥ Hairy Night Muddler Yellow ✥

Hook: Trailer tandem
    mount.
Thread: Black, red or
    yellow 4/0 or 6/0.
Treble hook body:
    Fluorescent green floss.
Tail: Yellow deer body
    hair.
Body: Preformed of yellow deer body hair.

Tying the Night Muddler Yellow
(Diagrams 5.7 and 5.8)

Step 1: Place the treble hook in the vise's jaws.
Step 2: Using yellow thread, form a firm foundation on the shank of the treble. Tie in the green fluorescent floss and form a body with it, tying it off at the base of the eye with the tying thread. Form a neat head, whip finish and varnish. Note: There is no dressing on the nylon connecting the hooks.
Step 3: Exchange the treble for the front hook in the vise's jaws.
Step 4: Wind the tying thread along the shank of the front hook to its bend. Construct a "hair hackle" of yellow

deer body hair and make 2 turns of it. Tie in and half hitch. Now tie in the preformed deer-hair dubbing brush, wind the thread forward to the hook's eye. Then with touching turns wrap the dubbing brush forward to the eye. Tie in.
Step 5: Form a neat head, whip finish and varnish.
Step 6: Trim the body into a cylinder shape, then taper the back down from head to tail. Flatten the under side of the body and varnish it.

I now move on to the flies and their variants that started me tying the Hairys. The first are low-water patterns for sea trout, salmon and steelhead. They are, in reality, Spey-type flies sparsely dressed with very short tails (if there is one), wings and hackles. In Britain they are tied on singles, doubles and even trebles on sizes 6 to 16, and are usually fished during the day in low-water conditions. Made with "hair hackles" they have an attractive pulsating action which has proved so irresistible to fish. It is very important that their wings are correctly tied.

My method of tying wings is now set forth. Remember wings should always be fairly sparse and must never be sticking up in the air, bunched on top of the hook. All wings should be tent shaped, less so in low water and Spey patterns, and more so in shrimp and Practitioner patterns. To achieve a secure tent-shaped wing, make 3 to 5 tight turns of thread over the wing fibres to bed them down on the thread-covered hook shank. Lift the butts of the wing material, and lock it in, with 2 turns of thread under the fibres tight against the hair and the first turns of thread. Now make 2 turns over the fibres in front of the locking threads. Use a finger-nail to spread the fibres around the top and down the sides of the body. To set the wings at the correct angle (± 30 degrees), wind the thread back over the wing fibres until they are lying at the required angle above the body, half hitch a couple of times.

The following pattern is an example of a low-water fly for sea trout.

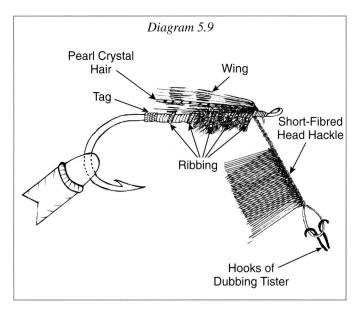

Diagram 5.9

- Pearl Crystal Hair
- Wing
- Tag
- Short-Fibred Head Hackle
- Ribbing
- Hooks of Dubbing Tister

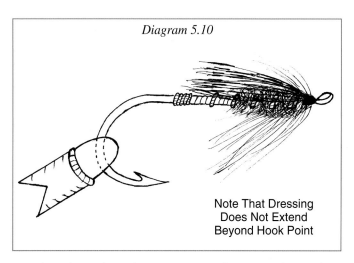

Diagram 5.10

Note That Dressing Does Not Extend Beyond Hook Point

❧ Hairy Gold Peter Ross ❧

Hook: Partridge 01 sizes 6-14.
Thread: Black 6/0 or 8/0.
Tail: None.
Ribbing: Gold oval tinsel.
Body: Rear 1/2 flat gold tinsel. Front 1/2 red fur dubbing.

Wing: Grey speckled hair from the base of a grey squirrel's tail and 2 strands of pearl crystal hair.
Hackle: Black hair.

Tying the Hairy Gold Peter Ross
(Diagrams 5.9 and 5.10)

Step 1: Place the hook in the vise's jaws.

Step 2: Starting 1 1/2 eye lengths from the eye, wind the tying thread back along the shank in tight touching turns to above the point of the hook. As I wind the thread back I usually catch in the ribbing and the flat gold tinsel about halfway along the shank. This gives a smooth foundation on which to wind the tinsel. (A tip, the short end of the flat tinsel should be facing towards the hook's bend.) Full flat tinsel bodies can also be formed in this fashion.

Step 3: Wind the tying thread back to where you tied in the tinsels. Wrap the flat tinsel back to above the point of the hook, and forward again to where you started from. Tie in and half hitch. Form a dubbing body on the front of the shank ending 2 eye lengths from the eye. Spiral 5 turns of ribbing over the whole body and tie in.

Step 4: Tie on the wings using my method described previously. The fibre tips should reach to just above the hook point and the wing should lie fairly close to the body.

Step 5: Construct a "hair hackle" with fibre length equal to the distance from the eye to the point of the hook. Wrap it forward, tie in and half hitch.

Step 6: Form a small neat head, whip finish and varnish.

Spey flies originated in the Spey valley of north east Scotland and date from the end of the 18th century. They are thought to have been amongst the first salmon flies tied in Scotland. Originally they were dressed with very long-fibred cock saddle hackles or with hackles from the blue heron (now protected). Recently natural and dyed saddle hackles from members of the pheasant family have taken the place of the traditional hackles. And now I have replaced feathers with hair. In Scotland, shrimp flies have now more or less taken over from the traditional hair-wing and Spey-style salmon flies. I am certain that the original Spey flies represented shrimp and that was why they were so effective. They are still if you fish with them, as do the steelhead fishermen of western North America. The likeness to shrimp can be seen if you hold down the materials against the hook shank and look at the resultant silhouette.

Their popularity among steelheaders is borne out by the number of new Spey fly patterns that appear each year.

Before embarking on how to tie Spey flies it is useful to define the component parts of the fly and their dimensions.

Tag: This is formed by winding 2 to 5 turns of flat, around or oval tinsel over the hook shank from opposite the base of the barb to opposite the hook point.

Tail: In the case of the Hairys, tails are usually short hair hackles with fibre lengths equal to 1/4 to 1/2 the length of the hook shank, this is especially true in the case of "Hairy Speys".

Ribbing: Strands of thread, wire, oval and flat tinsel spiralled over the body in equally spaced turns.

Body: Traditionally it stretches from the bend of the hook to about 3 eye lengths from the eye. It is often divided into fractions of different colours or materials.

Hackles: The fibre length in palmer hackles is important in Spey flies, and should be between 1 1/2 to 2 1/2 times the total length of the hook.

Wing length: In Spey flies the tips of the fibres making up the wing should end up opposite the bend of the hook.

Collar hackle: In Spey flies, unless otherwise stated, the length of hackle fibres should be 1 1/2 times the width of the hook's gape.

The following pattern is an example of a "Hairy" Spey:

❧ Hairy Bedsprings Spey ❧

Hook: Partridge CS10/2, Daiichi 2161 sizes 2-6.

Thread: Orange or red 6/0.

Tag: Flat gold tinsel and orange fluorescent floss.

Tail: Orange hair.

Ribbing: Fine flat gold tinsel.

Body: Rear 1/2 dubbed orange fur. Front 1/2 dubbed brown fur.

Body hackle: Preformed natural grey based black squirrel palmered over the front 1/2 of the body.

Wing: Hair from natural black or red Russian squirrel tails. (Substitute for bronze mallard.)

Collar hackle: Fox squirrel tail dyed fiery brown.

Head: Orange or red varnish.

Tying the Hairy Bedsprings Spey
(Diagrams 5.11 and 5.12)

Step 1: Place the hook in the vise's jaws.

Step 2: Form a thread foundation stretching along the shank from 2 eye lengths from the eye to above the hook's point.

Step 3: Tie in the tinsel. Wrap it back to above the base of the barb and forward again to above the hook point. Half hitch and tie in the floss for the second half of the tag. Wrap the floss back along the shank to above halfway between barb and the hook point and forward again to above the hook point, and tie off.

Step 4: Construct a sparse "hair hackle" for the tail and wind 1 turn and tie in.

Step 5: Tie in the ribbing dub the rear 1/2 of the body and tie in. Tie in the preformed Spey-style hackle and dub the front 1/2 of the body. Rib the body with 5 spirals of tinsel and tie off. Palmer the Spey hackle forward between the ribbing.

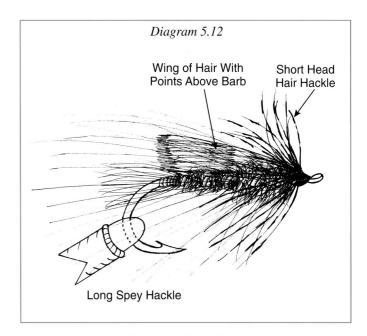

Diagram 5.12

Wing of Hair With Points Above Barb

Short Head Hair Hackle

Long Spey Hackle

Step 6: Tie in a slightly tent-shaped wing.

Step 7: Construct the collar hackle and make 2 turns of it and tie off.

Step 8: Form a neat small head, whip finish and varnish with red or orange lacquer.

After I had dressed the first "Hairy" Speys, and they had proved themselves, I decided to turn tried-and-tested hair-winged salmon flies into "Hairy" salmon flies. For inspiration I looked through my fly boxes and there in front of me were the answers, Waddingtons and tube flies. Thus "Hairy" Spey flies without wings became "Hairy" salmon flies which are very similar to Leggys. Then followed "Hairy" shrimps derived from the famous Scottish and Irish shrimp patterns such as the Ally's Shrimp. I am including definitions and dimensions of the various parts of these flies to help you dress them proportionally correct.

Tail: A sparse "hair hackle" made from hair, fur or synthetics. In salmon and tube flies, its fibre length should be between 1/2 and 3/4 of the shank's length. In shrimp patterns the fibre length should be equal to the overall length of the hook.

Palmered hackle: A "hair hackle" doubled and palmered in the normal way along the body. In salmon flies, its fibre length should be 1 1/2 times the width of the hook's gape.

Trailing hackle: A "hair hackle" 1 1/2 times the overall length of the hook. This hackle is equivalent to a salmon fly's wing.

Middle hackle: A "hair hackle" tied between the 2 halves of the body. The length of its fibres should be just over 1/2 the overall length of the hook.

Wings: In shrimp patterns, a bunch of black-tipped hair is substituted for jungle cock feathers. Or in the case of Ally's Shrimp, black-tipped hair dyed orange is substituted for golden pheasant tippets.

Front hackle: This "hair hackle" is always tied in front of the wings. Its fibre length should be 1 1/2 times the width

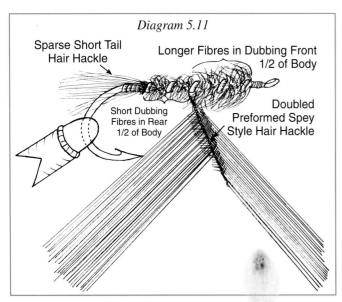

Diagram 5.11

Sparse Short Tail Hair Hackle

Longer Fibres in Dubbing Front 1/2 of Body

Short Dubbing Fibres in Rear 1/2 of Body

Doubled Preformed Spey Style Hair Hackle

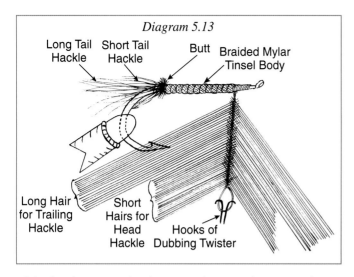

Diagram 5.13

Long Tail Hackle
Short Tail Hackle
Butt
Braided Mylar Tinsel Body
Long Hair for Trailing Hackle
Short Hairs for Head Hackle
Hooks of Dubbing Twister

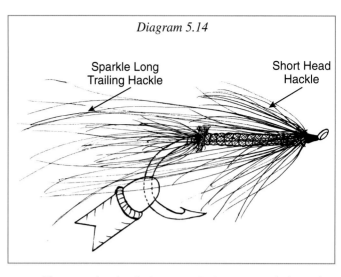

Diagram 5.14

Sparkle Long Trailing Hackle
Short Head Hackle

of the hook's gape. The dressing of a typical "Hairy" salmon fly is now given. This dressing can also be used for tube flies and Waddingtons.

❧ Dunkeld ❧

Hook: Partridge M, TMC 7999, Daiichi 2441 sizes 4-12.
Thread: Yellow or orange 6/0 or 8/0.
Tag: Flat or oval gold tinsel.
Tail: Yellow Antron wool under red Antron wool.
Butt: Black ostrich herl.
Body: Embossed gold braided Mylar tinsel.
Trailing hackle: Grey squirrel tail hairs dyed orange.
Front hackle: Hot orange hair.

Tying the Dunkeld (Diagrams 5.13 and 5.14)
Step 1: Place the hook in the vise's jaws.
Step 2: Form a firm thread foundation stretching along the shank 2 eye lengths from the eye to a point above the barb of the hook.
Step 3: Form the tag and in front of it, a dubbing loop, into which you'll insert the yellow Antron fibres of correct tail length followed by red Antron fibres 1/2 the length of the yellow ones. Spin the dubbing twister, double the hackle and wind 2 turns of it forward.
Step 4: Tie in the ostrich herl and form the butt.
Step 5: Tie in the braided Mylar and wrap it forward to 3 eye lengths from the eye, and tie in.
Step 6: In one dubbing loop insert the hairs of the trailing hackle and the front hackle form the combined hackles and wind them forward to 1 eye length from the eye, and tie off.
Step 7: Form a neat head, whip finish and varnish.

Most Hairys can be dressed as tube flies. They are tied on aluminum, brass, copper or plastic tubes in lengths from 1/4 inch to 2 1/2 inches. To prevent the

monofilament leader being cut, it is essential that aluminum, brass and copper tubes are plastic lined. Tube flies tied with "Hair hackles" are durable, neater, have small heads and that great pulsating action in the water. I use a tube-fly attachment on my vise to tie them, but a hook with its eye cut off placed in a vise is quite adequate. You merely have to push the tube onto an eyeless hook shank of the correct diameter.

❧ Hairy Willie Gunn Tube Fly ❧

Thread: Black 6/0 or 8/0.
Ribbing: Flat gold tinsel.
Body: Black floss varnished.
Hackle: Mixed yellow, orange and black hair.

Tying the Hairy Willie Gunn Tube Fly
Step 1: Push tube onto eyeless hook.
Step 2: Form a firm thread base on the tube.
Step 3: Tie in ribbing and floss.
Step 4: Wrap tying thread forward to 1/16 of an inch from front end of tube. Then wrap floss forward to same point and tie off. Varnish body with clear lacquer.
Step 5: Rib body, tie in, re-varnish, remove the tube and allow it to dry.
Step 6: Replace tube on the hook shank and construct a "hair hackle".
Step 7: Wrap hackle, tie off, form a small head, whip finish and varnish.

The penultimate fly in this chapter is the Hairy Shrimp. The feather versions of shrimp flies are the most popular salmon flies fished with in Scotland and Ireland. Consequently most fish are caught on them. The pulsating action of the Hairy Shrimps has led to even greater prominence being given to shrimp flies. The following pattern in its original dressing is world famous. The Hairy version is as good!

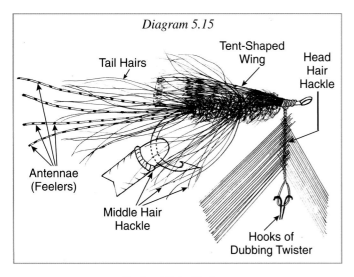

Diagram 5.15

Tail Hairs

Tent-Shaped Wing

Head Hair Hackle

Antennae (Feelers)

Middle Hair Hackle

Hooks of Dubbing Twister

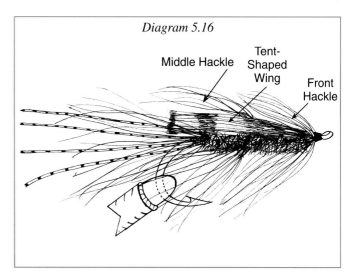

Diagram 5.16

Middle Hackle

Tent-Shaped Wing

Front Hackle

❧ Hairy Ally's Shrimp ❧

Hook: Single, double or treble salmon irons.
Thread: Red 6/0 or 8/0.
Tag: Oval gold tinsel.
Feelers: 4 strands of pearl crystal hair.
Tail: Orange hair (sparse).
Ribbing: Oval gold tinsel.
Rear Body: Red floss or fur dubbing.
Middle hackle: Grey squirrel tail hairs.
Ribbing: Oval gold tinsel.
Front body: Black fur dubbing.
Wing: Black-tipped woodchuck dyed hot orange.
Front hackle: Dyed orange hair.
Head: Red varnish.

Tying the Hairy Ally's Shrimp
(Diagrams 5.15 and 5.16)

Step 1: Place the hook in the vise's jaws.
Step 2: Form a firm foundation along the shank stretching from an eye's length from the eye to the bend of the hook.
Step 3: Form a tag with 3 to 5 turns of tinsel.
Step 4: Tie in 4 strands of crystal hair equal to 2 shank lengths.
Step 5: Construct a sparse "hair hackle" of orange hair and make 1 turn of it.
Step 6: Tie in the ribbing and form the rear 1/2 body of red fur dubbing. Rib the body with 3 turns of tinsel.
Step 7: Construct the middle hackle and wrap 1 turn of it.
Step 8: Tie in the ribbing for the front body. Dub the front 1/2 of the body with black fur, and rib it with 3 turns of the oval tinsel.
Step 9: Tie in a tent-shaped wing whose tips reach to above the hook's bend.
Step 10: Construct the front hackle, winf it forward and tie off.
Step 11: Form a neat head, whip finish and varnish with red lacquer.

A set of Hairy Practitioners in various sizes, tied on single and double hooks, is all that is required to catch salmon, steelhead and sea trout in Europe and North America. I have been pleasantly surprised at the number I have had to tie for friends and clients who swear that they are the best flies they have fished with for a long time. There is no doubt that they are taken for shrimp, as one look at them immediately shows the resemblance. They are not the easiest of flies to tie but are well worth the battle. Just remember that they must look streamlined and shrimp like. I hope the following notes and tips on tying them will help you.

Tails: Must be made with fibres of the correct length. The crystal-hair feelers must be 1 1/2 times the total hook length. (Bend to eye of the hook.) The long "hair hackle" must be 1 to 1 1/2 times the hook length. The fibres of the second "hair hackle" must be 1/2 the length of the first tail hackle.

Tip: When tying tail or any "hair hackles", pull them tight against the hook shank. This makes the fibres stick out. Two turns of thread over the base of the hackle will slant it slightly backwards.

Eyes: Eyes must stick outwards and slightly upwards with their bulbs just past the hook's bend, so that the rear wing can lie in between them.

Ribbing and body: The tinsel ribbing must be evenly spaced, 2 1/2 turns for each half of the body. The dubbing must be well pricked out, especially on the rear half of he body.

Tip: I brush out the dubbing before ribbing, using a brass gun-cleaning brush. I prick out again after ribbing.

Wings: Both rear and front wings must be spread tent-like around the top half of the hook shank. This makes them less bunched on top of the hook and enables them to lie flatter along the top of the body, and allows quivering action in the water. When hair is bunched too thickly it will not move.

Tip: When tying in hair, make 4 or 5 tight turns around the hair and the hook shank making sure that the hair is tied on top of a thread base. Push the hair down with a finger or thumb nail spreading it around the top half of the body. Make 3 or 4 more tight turns of thread. Lift the butt ends of the hair and make 2 or 3 turns tight up against the hair. Now make 2 or 3 turns over the hair in front of the locking turns, cut off the butts of the hair. Make several turns of

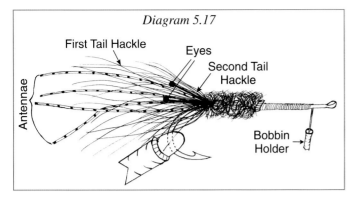

Diagram 5.17

First Tail Hackle
Eyes
Second Tail Hackle
Antennae
Bobbin Holder

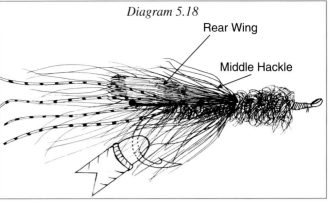

Diagram 5.18

Rear Wing
Middle Hackle

thread back over the hair towards the hook's bend. This should lay the hair flatter over the body.

Hair hackles: In the middle hackle, the tips of the fibres must reach just beyond the bend of the hook. In the front hackle, the fibre tips must reach to the hook's point.

Tips: It is important to spread the hair in the dubbing loop evenly along the strands of the dubbing loop. The hairs must not cross each other. Before spinning the dubbing loop, adjust the fibres to the correct length. Cut the butt ends to between 1/16 and 1/8 of an inch from the dubbing loop threads. Spin the loop and double the hackle. Stroke the hackle fibres back while winding the hackle towards the hook's eye. Two tight turns of thread over the base of the hackle will slope it back at the correct angle.

All the Practitioners catch fish but the one that is described below is a favourite of steelhead fly fishermen.

❧ Solduc Hairy Practitioner ❧

Hook: Single: Partridge CS10/1 sizes 1-8. Double: Partridge Q sizes 2-12.

Thread: Orange or yellow 6/0 or 8/0.

Tag: Oval silver tinsel.

Antennae: 4 strands of pearl crystal hair.

Tail: First hackle: Grey squirrel tail dyed yellow. Second hackle: Dyed orange hair.

Eyes: Black mono eyes.

Ribbing: Oval silver tinsel.

Body: Rear half: Fluorescent orange dubbing.

Rear wing: Dyed orange hair.

Middle hackle: Yellow hair.

Body: Front half: Hot orange dubbing.

Front wing: Grey squirrel tail dyed orange.

Head hackle: Black hair.

Head: Red lacquer.

Tying the Solduc Hairy Practitioner
(Diagrams 5.17, 5.18 and 5.19)

Step 1: Place the hook in the vise's jaws.

Step 2: Run the tying thread back to the hook's bend.

Step 3: Tie in the oval silver tinsel and form a tag.

Step 4: For the antennae, tie in 4 strands of pearl crystal hair. The length of the antennae equals twice the shank length.

Step 5: Insert into a dubbing loop the fibres required for the 2 tail hackles. The length of fibre for the first hackle equal to the overall length of the hook. The length of the fibres in the second hackle is 1/2 that of those in the first.

Step 6: Tie in the eyes. These should be tied in each side of the hook shank and protrude just beyond the hook's bend.

Step 7: Tie in the ribbing. Dub the rear half of the body and over it spiral 2 1/2 turns of the tinsel and tie in.

Step 8: Tie on the rear wing of squirrel tail to lie flat and tent shaped over the rear body. The tips of the fibres protruding a little beyond the eyes and in between them, thus forming the front half of the carapace.

Step 9: Construct and tie in the middle hackle, the fibres of which should reach to just past the hooks bend.

Step 10: Tie in the ribbing again and dub the front half of the body. Spiral 2 1/2 turns of the tinsel over the body and tie off.

Step 11: Tie in the tent-shaped front wing flat on top of the body. The tips of the wing's fibres should come to just above the hook's point.

Step 12: Construct the head hackle with fibre length 1 1/2 times the hook's gape and wrap 1 turn of it and tie off.

Step 13: Form a small neat head, whip finish and varnish.

Many patterns such as those listed under trout flies and bass bugs can be used for salmon, steelhead and sea trout. It is best to leave it to you, the reader, to experiment and find that irresistible fly. I suggest that you start with dyed fox fur as a substitute for marabou in steelhead flies.

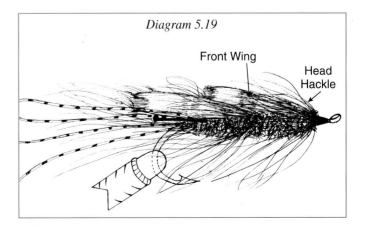

Diagram 5.19

Front Wing
Head Hackle

Chapter 6

Bass & Pike Bugs

Over the past 50 years I have developed a range of bass bugs and flies that have proved to be successful in catching largemouth and smallmouth bass in many countries of the world. Recently I have changed many of my patterns made of feathers or a combination of hair and feathers to pure Hairys, and these are the ones I put forward for you to tie and try out. Many of these creations are used in the U.K. and Europe for bream, chub, perch, pike, taimen and zander. Their versatility goes further. Modified versions have taken sea fish, and the mini variants have accounted for the taking of all species of trout and panfish.

The techniques involved are those explained in chapters 4 and 5 and are mainly modifications to "hair hackles". The following are the most important ones.

1. Formation of "Hair Hackle" Extended Bodies
Method (Diagrams 6.1 and 6.2).

Step 1: Construct a "hair hackle" at the hook's bend for nymphs, or at the middle of the shank for extended bodies of craneflies, damselflies and various mayflies.

Step 2: Stroke the hackle fibres back, lift them upwards and make 2 or 3 turns of thread under them on the hook shank so that all the fibres are above it. Now make 3 or 4 turns of thread over the fibres and around the hook shank, and secure with 2 half hitches. Cut off the thread.

Step 3: Hold the fibres of the "hair hackle" together with a clip or hackle pliers. Slip a double half hitch over the ends of the fibres. Place the knot 1/4 inch from the tips and tighten it. Make several more turns of thread and 2 half hitches to form the first rib of the segmented body. Cut off the thread. In similar fashion, form 4 more equally spaced bindings for the ribs of the body.

Step 4: The rest of the fly can now be tied.

⤜ Hairy Olive Damsel Nymph (Extended body) ⤛

Hook: Any 2x-long nymph hook wtd. Your choice.

Thread: Dark green 6/0.

Weight: Copper or lead wire.

Eyes: Mono nymph eyes painted black.

Tail: Olive arctic fox fur "hair hackle" segmented with tying thread.

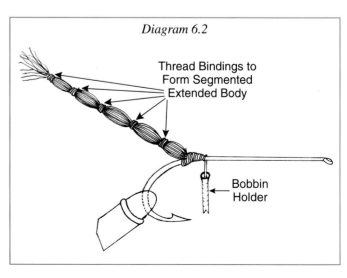

Thorax: Olive fur dubbing.

Hackle: Dyed olive arctic fox tail fibres.

Head: Brown dubbing.

Tying the Hairy Olive Damsel Nymph (Extended Body)
(Diagrams 6.3 and 6.4)

Step 1: Place the hook in the vise's jaws.

Step 2: Form a firm thread foundation from the eye back to the bend of the hook.

Step 3: Weight the hook by the keel method over 3/4 of the shank.

Diagram 6.1

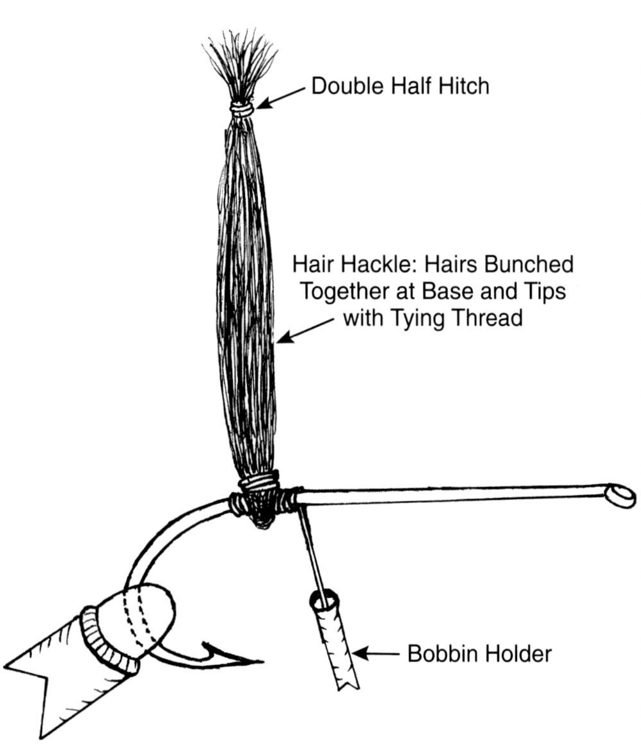

- Double Half Hitch
- Hair Hackle: Hairs Bunched Together at Base and Tips with Tying Thread
- Bobbin Holder

Diagram 6.2

- Thread Bindings to Form Segmented Extended Body
- Bobbin Holder

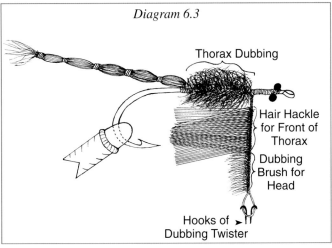

Diagram 6.3

Thorax Dubbing

Hair Hackle for Front of Thorax

Dubbing Brush for Head

Hooks of Dubbing Twister

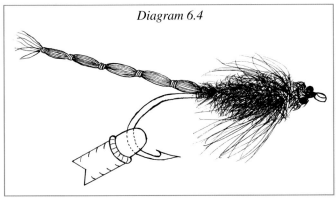

Diagram 6.4

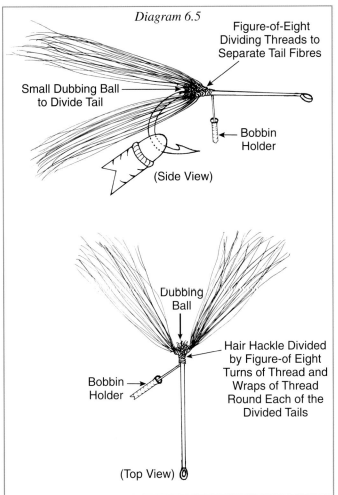

Diagram 6.5

Figure-of-Eight Dividing Threads to Separate Tail Fibres

Small Dubbing Ball to Divide Tail

Bobbin Holder

(Side View)

Dubbing Ball

Bobbin Holder

Hair Hackle Divided by Figure-of Eight Turns of Thread and Wraps of Thread Round Each of the Divided Tails

(Top View)

Step 4: Tie in the mono nymph eyes with figure-of-eight bindings 1 1/2 eyes lengths from the eye.

Step 5: Run the thread back to the bend and construct a "hair hackle" of olive fox fur with fibre length equal to 1 1/4 that of the shank's length. Follow step 2 in methods of forming extended bodies.

Step 6: Form a well pricked out, dubbed thorax tying it off 3 eye lengths from the eye.

Step 7: Construct a "hair hackle" of olive fox tail with fibre length equal to the hook's gape. Wind it forward and tie off behind the eyes.

Step 8: Form a brown fur dubbed head using figure-of-eight bindings around the eyes. Tie off.

Step 9: Form a small head, whip finish and varnish.

2. Formation of "hair hackle" Legs, Wings and Feelers Method (Diagrams 6.5 and 6.6).

Step 1: Construct a "hair hackle" at a point on the hook's shank where you want to place the legs, wings or feelers.

Step 2: Carefully divide the hackle into 2 equal bunches with figure-of-eight bindings.

(a) For legs and feelers: Make 2 or 3 turns of thread around the divided fibres close up against the hook on either side of the shank. This will help keep the legs sticking outwards. Bends in the legs or feelers can be fashioned later.

(b) For wings: Stroke the fibres of the "hair hackle" back and holding their tips well above the hook, make 3 or 4 turns of thread under them on the shank tight up against the base of the hackle. Still holding the fibres upwards, make 2 or 3 turns of thread around them to lift them above the hook shank. Divide the bunch of fibres into 2 equal parts with figure-of-eight bindings over the base of the hackle and the hook's shank. Tie off and half hitch. If need be, use thread bindings of various types to set wing angles.

My first successful bass fly was the Hairy Fairy which I invented in 1957 and in 1979 was incorporated into the name of a fly-tying firm with which I was associated. The original was part hair and part feather. It is basically a palmer with a divided tail made of hair. The pattern given next is made totally of hair and fur.

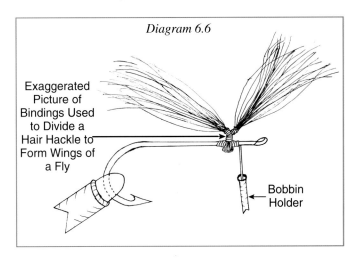

Diagram 6.6

Exaggerated Picture of Bindings Used to Divide a Hair Hackle to Form Wings of a Fly

Bobbin Holder

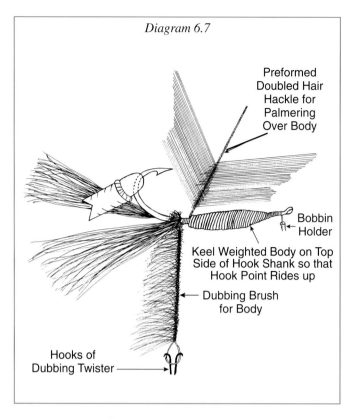

Diagram 6.7

Preformed Doubled Hair Hackle for Palmering Over Body

Bobbin Holder

Keel Weighted Body on Top Side of Hook Shank so that Hook Point Rides up

Dubbing Brush for Body

Hooks of Dubbing Twister

⊰ The Hairy Grey Hairy Fairy ⊱

Hook: TMC 5262, Partridge D4A, Mustad 9671, Daiichi 1710. Bass sizes 2 and 4 wtd. Trout sizes 6-10 wtd.

Thread: Black 6/0 or 8/0.

Underbody: White floss.

Weight: Lead or heavy copper wire. Keel on top of shank.

Tail: Grey squirrel tail hairs.

Body: Grey fur dubbing brush. (Grey squirrel body fur makes a very nice body.)

Body hackle: Preformed "hair hackle" of grey squirrel tail palmered.

Head hackle: Grey fox tail.

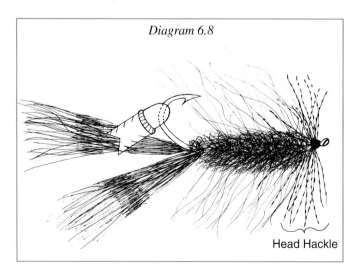

Diagram 6.8

Head Hackle

Tying the Hairy Grey Hairy Fairy

(Diagrams 6. 7 and 6.8)

Step 1: Place the hook in the vise's jaws.

Step 2: Form a firm thread foundation stretching from the eye to the bend of the hook.

Step 3: Tie in the floss and form a torpedo-shaped body.

Step 4: Weight the fly by the keel method with the initial keel lying along the top side of the shank so the point rides up. The keel shape should be pronounced due to the torpedo underbody.

Step 5: At the hook's bend construct a fairly dense "hair hackle" with fibre lengths equal to the overall length of the hook. Divide the hackle into 2 equal bunches using figure-of-eight bindings. [See Formation of "Hair Hackle" Legs, Method 2 (a) page 22].

Step 6: Tie in preformed hackle. Its fibre lengths should be equal to the shank's length.

Step 7: Form dubbing brush of fur and wrap it forward to 2 eye lengths from the eye.

Step 8: Palmer the body hackle forward and tie in.

Step 9: Construct the head "hair hackle" with fibre length equal to the overall length of the body. Wrap the hackle forward and tie off 1 eye length from the eye.

Step 10: Form a neat head, whip finish and varnish.

⊰ Hairy Mouse ⊱

Hook: TMC 8089, Mustad 80300BR, Daiichi 2720 sizes 2-10.

Thread: Black or yellow 6/0.

Tail support: A 25-pound monofilament loop.

Tail: Black or brown leather strip 2 1/2 times the length of the hook's shank tapered from

3/16 inch at the base to 3/32 inch at the tip of the tail.

Body: A premade "hair hackle" of natural grey/brown deer hair.

Ears: A pair of shaped leather ears.

Head: Spun or stacked natural deer hair cut to shape.

Eyes: Black plastic beads cut in half.

Whiskers: Black squirrel tail hairs.

Weed guard: Very thin tungsten wire loop preformed to the correct length.

Tying the Hairy Mouse (Diagram 6.9).

Step 1: Place the hook in the vise's jaws.

Step 2: From 1/3 of the hook shank from the eye to the bend of the hook, form a firm thread foundation. Bind in the strand of monofilament along the near side of the shank, make a loop at the hook's bend equal in length to 1/4 of the hook's shank and bind in the other end of the loop along the far side of the shank. Narrow the loop to width of the tail by binding the tying thread along it.

Step 3: Tie in the prepared leather tail. Put a drop of glue on the bindings under the tail and on the mono loop before tying it in.

Hair-Hackle Tying Techniques & Fly Patterns

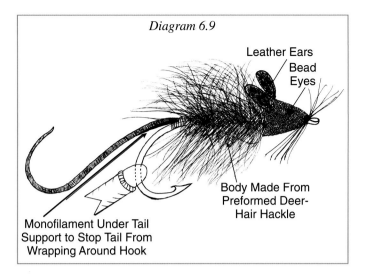

Diagram 6.9

Leather Ears

Bead Eyes

Body Made From Preformed Deer-Hair Hackle

Monofilament Under Tail Support to Stop Tail From Wrapping Around Hook

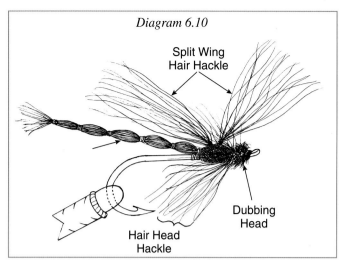

Diagram 6.10

Split Wing Hair Hackle

Dubbing Head

Hair Head Hackle

Step 4: Tie in the preformed deer-hair "hair hackle". Make certain that the hackle fibres are equal to the length of the hook shank. Wrap the "hair hackle" forward pushing the turns of it close together with a hair packer. Finish at the point where you started the thread foundation. Tie in and half hitch.

Step 5: Tie in the ears pushing them tight up against the deer-hair body.

Step 6: Tie in the weed guard. Adjust to the correct length. The loop end should rest on the hook point in front of the barb and the open ends must pass through the hook's eye leaving enough of the ends to tie in on top of the shank. Lift the loop of the hook point to allow for the spinning of a deer hair head.

Step 7: Spin or stack a tightly packed deer-hair head and trim to shape.

Step 8: Burn 2 eye sockets into the deer-hair and glue in the half beads.

Step 9: Tie in the whiskers with tight figure-of-eight bindings. Bend the wire back to rest on the hook point and form a head over it. Whip finish and varnish.

⋙ Hairy Damsel Fly (Spent style) ⋘

Hook: Preferred Partridge 01 sizes 6-12. Similar sizes in TMC 8089, Mustad 80300BR or Daiichi 2720.

Thread: Black 6/0.

Eyes: Mono nymph eyes painted black.

Body: Dyed blue deer hair or bucktail.

Ribbing: Black tying thread.

Wings: Dyed grey deer hair with a few dyed blue deer-hair fibres mixed in.

Thorax: Dubbing brush of dyed-blue deer hair trimmed to shape.

Hackle: Sparse black squirrel tail.

Head: Black dubbing.

Tying the Hairy Damsel Fly (Spent style)
(Diagram 6.10)

Step 1: Place hook in vise's jaws.

Step 2: Form a firm base of tying thread starting 1 eye length from the eye and ending half-way along the shank. Wind the thread forward to within 2 eye lengths from the eye, and tie in the eyes with figure-of-eight bindings. Return the thread to the mid point of the shank.

Step 3: Form an extended body. (Refer back to formation of "hair hackle" extended bodies number 3 of method.) The length of the hackle fibres should equal 1 1/4 the shank's length.

Step 4: Construct a "hair hackle" for the wings with fibre length equal to 1 1/2 the shank's length. Follow the instructions given in Step 2(b) of the Method of Formation of "Hair Hackle" Wings,"

Step 5: Form the thorax with a dubbing brush of blue deer hair. Tie off the dubbing brush 1/4 of the shank's length from the eye. Trim the thorax to shape.

Step 6: Construct a sparse "hair hackle" with fibre length 3/4 the length of the shank. Wrap it forward and tie off.

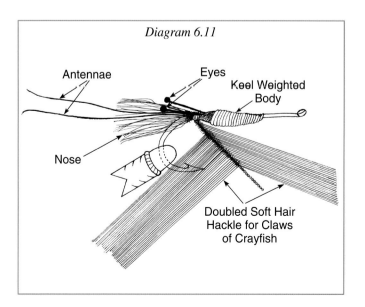

Diagram 6.11

Antennae

Eyes

Keel Weighted Body

Nose

Doubled Soft Hair Hackle for Claws of Crayfish

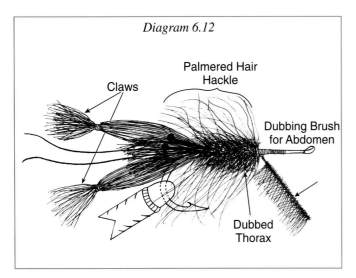

Diagram 6.12

Claws · Palmered Hair Hackle · Dubbing Brush for Abdomen · Dubbed Thorax

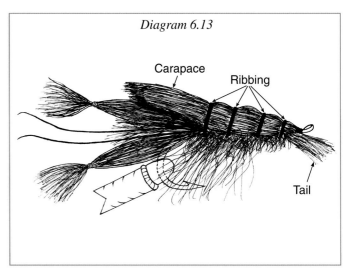

Diagram 6.13

Carapace · Ribbing · Tail

Step 7: Construct a black fur dubbing brush and wrap it forward around the eyes to form the head. Tie off.

Step 8: Form a neat head, whip finish and varnish.

The next bug incorporates most of the techniques used in the Hairys. Tied on a stainless hook it represents many crustaceans found in the sea. It is time-consuming to tie but is well worth the effort and looks good in a fly-box. In fresh water it is a killer for most fish, particularly bass and large trout.

⇔ Hairy Brown Crayfish ⇔

Hook: Partridge N, Mustad 90240, TMC 7989, Daiichi 2421 sizes 2-6 wtd.

Thread: Colour to blend with body material.

Underbody: Floss silk to build up thorax slightly.

Weight: Lead or copper wire.

Antennae: Fine black bucktail or elk mane.

Nose: Short, fairly thick "hair hackle" of dyed fiery brown squirrel tail.

Eyes: 30-pound melted monofilament dipped in black varnish to make stalk eyes.

Claws: "Hair Hackle" of dyed brown opossum or raccoon fur.

Ribbing: Clear monofilament.

Thorax hackle: Woodchuck guard hairs dyed fiery brown.

Thorax: Ginger fur dubbing.

Abdomen: Ginger fur dubbing.

Carapace: Fox squirrel tail dyed fiery brown coated with Softex and epoxy.

Tail: The butt ends of the carapace coated with Softex.

Tying the Hairy Brown Crayfish
(Diagrams 6.11, 6.12 and 6.13)

Step 1: Place the hook in the vise's jaws.

Step 2: Form a firm foundation of tying thread stretching along the shank of the hook 1 eye length from the eye to the hook's bend. I varnish the foundation to strengthen it.

Step 3: Tie in the floss. Build up the thorax in front of the hook's point and taper the abdomen towards the eye.

Step 4: Using the keel method, weight the hook under the shank.

Step 5: At the hook's bend, tie in the 2 hairs for the antennae. Their length equal to twice that of the hook's shank.

Step 6: Still at the bend of the hook, construct a fairly heavy "hair hackle" of dyed squirrel tail with fibre length equal to 1/2 the shank's length. Wrap it forward and make 3 or 4 turns of thread over its base to form the nose.

Step 7: Tie in the stalk eyes on either side of the shank. They should protrude to above the hook's bend.

Step 8: Above the hook's point, construct a "hair hackle" of dyed brown arctic fox or raccoon fur with fibre length equal to 1 1/2 the shank's length. Form the claws by dividing the hackle into 2 equal bunches with figure-of-eight bindings. These should stick out either side of the nose. Place double half hitches on each bunch at a point 2/3 of the fibre length from their base. Using the double half hitch as a base to work from, make a short binding to form each of the claws. Varnish the bindings and allow them to dry before continuing. I suggest you tie four or more crayfish at a time. By the time you have finished the last one's claws the first one should be ready to complete. In fact, this is a bug that can be made in stages.

Step 9: Tie in the ribbing and form 2 dubbing loops. In the second loop, construct a fur dubbing brush for the thorax. Wrap it forward to the mid point of the shank and tie in. In the first loop, construct a "hair hackle" with fibre length equal to 1/2 the shank. Palmer the hackle forward to mid shank and tie in.

Step 10: Construct a fur dubbing brush for the abdomen and wrap it forward to 2 eye lengths from the eye, and tie off.

Step 11: Cut a bunch of fiery brown dyed squirrel tail hairs

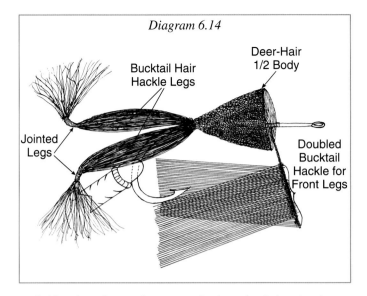

Diagram 6.14

Jointed Legs

Bucktail Hair Hackle Legs

Deer-Hair 1/2 Body

Doubled Bucktail Hackle for Front Legs

with fibre length equal to 1 1/2 the length of the shank. Tie in these hairs to form a tent-style wing over the abdomen and thorax to form the carapace. Do not cut off the butts of the hairs as these will form the fan-shaped tail.

Step 12: Rib over the thorax, abdomen and wing with the mono thread making sure that the thread is pulled tight into the materials to give a segmented effect. Tie in the ribbing thread. Spread the hair butts into a fan shape and form a small head under the fan.

Step 13: Coat the carapace with Softex or its equivalent. Let it dry thoroughly and then give it a thin final coat of epoxy.

Step 14: Trim the tail into a fan shape.

Artificial frogs are great favourites amongst bass fishermen, and the number of flies and bugs dressed to represent them is vast. The Hairy Fairy was originally tied as a frog pattern, although I am certain that it was taken by bass and trout for a freshwater crab. Crabs abound in the rivers and dams of South Africa and bass and trout love them. The "hair hackle" Legged Frog is merely a frog pattern with legs made from "hair hackles" instead of bunches of bucktail. The hair in "hair hackle" legs will not pull out

and there is little bulking up of tying thread making it easier to spin and stack deer hair around them.

The following frog pattern is a weedless shallow-running diver which has proved successful around reed beds and lily pads.

⊰⊱ **Weedless Hairy Legged Frog** ⊰⊱

Hook: TMC 8089, Mustad 80300BR, Daiichi 2720 sizes 2-10.

Thread: Yellow 6/0 for legs and 4/0 for tying deer hair.

Hind legs: Yellow bucktail "hair hackle" followed by olive bucktail "hair hackle" divided and jointed.

Body: Black, yellow and olive deer hair stacked over yellow and white deer hair trimmed to shape.

Front legs: Yellow bucktail "hair hackle" followed by olive bucktail "hair hackle" divided and jointed.

Head: Black, yellow and olive deer hair stacked over white deer hair trimmed to shape.

Eyes: Solid plastic eyes.

Weed guard: Thin stainless steel or tungsten wire loop.

Tying the Weedless Hairy Legged Frog
(Diagrams 6.14 and 6.15)

Note: this is a bug that is best made production fashion in stages, say six at a time.

Step 1: Place the hook in the vise's jaws.

Step 2: Form a thread foundation from halfway along the shank to above the hook point.

Step 3: Construct a yellow bucktail "hair hackle", divide it into 2 equal bunches with figure-of-eight bindings and tie off.

Step 4: Construct the second olive bucktail "hair hackle" close up against the yellow divided "hair hackle". Divide it with figure-of-eight turns over it and the yellow divided hackle. Try to get the olive hairs to lie on top of the yellow ones. Use brass lace-maker's pins to form the leg joints. Place the pin point first into the vise's jaws. From behind the head of the pin, form a 1/4-inch thread base. With the fibres jutting out 1/3 of their length beyond the pin's head, bind them in with tight touching turns from close up against the pin's head back to the end of the thread base, half hitch and whip finish. Repeat the process on the other leg. Varnish the joints and leave them to dry thoroughly. This is the end of the first stage.

Step 5: Form a tightly packed deer-hair body over the rear 1/2 of the shank. Trim to shape. Again it is best to stack the bodies of up to 6 bugs first then trim them. This helps you to make an almost identical batch of bugs, and makes you feel that you have achieved something.

Step 6: Construct 2 bucktail "hair hackles" for the front legs as in steps 3 and 4 above. Push the legs hard up against the body.

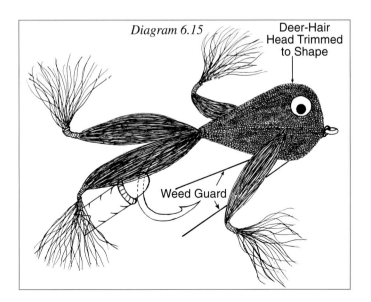

Diagram 6.15

Deer-Hair Head Trimmed to Shape

Weed Guard

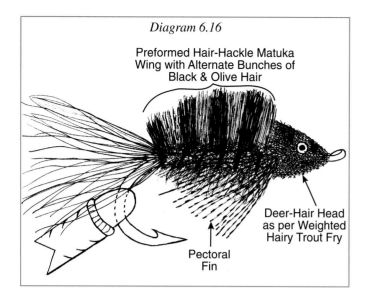

Diagram 6.16

Preformed Hair-Hackle Matuka
Wing with Alternate Bunches of
Black & Olive Hair

Deer-Hair Head
as per Weighted
Hairy Trout Fry

Pectoral
Fin

Step 7: Using the stacking method, form a tightly packed bulbous head on the front end of the shank. Form a small head and whip finish. Now trim to a bulb shape then cut a U-shaped groove sloping back from the centre of the eye at an angle of 45 degrees. Don't make the edges of the groove too narrow. Apply a lavish amount of varnish to the front of the head, especially to the groove.

Step 8: Burn eye sockets on each side of the head, and glue in the eyes.

Step 9: Construct a U-shaped stainless steel wire weed guard. (Diagram 6.16). This weed guard is attached by placing the bent U-shaped end under the hook's shank behind the eye and pushing its two ends through the eye from the top side. Bend the prongs of the weed-guard back.

The next bug is one of my fry patterns dressed on a large hook. In small sizes it can be used for trout and panfish. I make fry patterns in two styles, floating divers or deep-running sinkers. Thus these patterns can be fished throughout the season at any depth in the water.

❧ Hairy Yellow Perch Weighted ❧

Hook: Partridge N, Mustad 90240, TMC 7989 Daiichi 2421 sizes 1/0, 2 and 4 wtd.

Thread: Yellow 4/0 and 6/0.

Under body: White floss silk.

Weight: Lead wire.

Tail: Mixture of grey 70%, olive 25%, and orange 5% squirrel tail or woodchuck hair.

Ribbing: Clear monofilament.

Back Matuka hackle: Preformed "hair hackle" of alternate bunches of black and golden olive hairs or guard hairs.

Body: A mixture of fur dubbing; 60% cream and 40% bright yellow.

Pectoral fins: Dyed olive and orange squirrel tail hairs.

Gills: Dyed red fur dubbing.

Collar: Olive on top of golden olive over white deer hair.

Head: Olive stacked over golden olive and white deer hair trimmed to shape.

Eyes: Solid plastic.

Tying the Hairy Yellow Perch
(Diagram 6.16)

Step 1: Place the hook in the vise's jaws.

Step 2: Form a firm thread base over the rear 2/3 of the shank.

Step 3: Tie in the white floss silk and form a torpedo-shaped underbody.

Step 4: Weight the fly under the shank using the keel method.

Step 5: At the hook's bend construct a "hair hackle" of grey, olive and orange hair with fibre length equal to 3/4 of the hook's shank. Wrap it forward and tie off.

Step 6: Tie in the ribbing and the premade Matuka hackle.

Step 7: Form a dubbing brush of cream and yellow fur dubbing and wrap it forward to 1/3 of the shank's length from the eye. Tie in.

Step 8: Bring the premade Matuka hackle over the back of the body. Pull it tight into the body dubbing and tie in. Tightly spiral 5 turns of ribbing through the hackle to hold it in place. Tie off the ribbing and prick out the fur dubbing of the body and any Matuka hackle fibres caught under the ribbing.

Step 9: For the pectoral fins, construct a "hair hackle" of olive and orange squirrel tail hairs. The length of the hackle hairs should be equal to 1/2 the shank's length. Wind 2 turns of the hackle around the shank and with figure-of-eight bindings divide it so as the fibres stick out either side of the body to form the fins.

Step 10: Form a dubbing brush of dyed red fur. Figure-of-eight the brush around the pectoral fins to form the gills, and tie in.

Step 11: To form the collar, stack olive on top of golden olive over white deer body hair.

Step 12: Form the head of olive and golden olive stacked over white deer body hair. Trim to oval shape with flat sides and arounded top and bottom. Burn eye sockets into each side of the head and glue in the eyes. Varnish the front of the head.

This bug can also be tied on a keel hook to make it weedless. (See Chapter 4, Hairy Trout Flies.)

For the Floating Diving Yellow Perch, the tail, body, fins, gills and collar remain the same but the deer-hair head is sculptured as follows. Form the head of olive and golden olive deer body hair stacked over white deer hair. It is important to stack the deer hair along the sides of the hook shank as well as on top and underneath it. First cut the head into a cylinder shape which should slope slightly back and up from the eye to the collar. Using a razor blade,

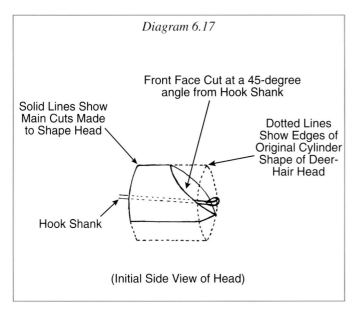

Diagram 6.17

Solid Lines Show
Main Cuts Made
to Shape Head

Front Face Cut at a 45-degree
angle from Hook Shank

Dotted Lines
Show Edges of
Original Cylinder
Shape of Deer-
Hair Head

Hook Shank

(Initial Side View of Head)

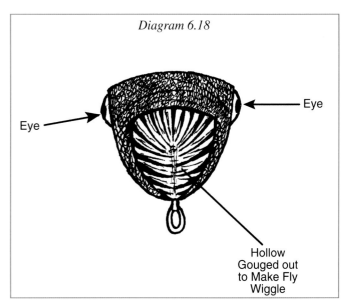

Diagram 6.18

Eye

Eye

Hollow
Gouged out
to Make Fly
Wiggle

cut a flat bottom to the head halfway between the hook shank and the edge of the cylinder. Now with a pair of scissors, cut a groove in the top half of the cylinder exactly over the middle of the hook shank, and sloping at a 45-degree angle from the base of the eye to the top of cylinder. Widen the groove carefully to form a "U"-shaped front to the head. Varnish the front and bottom of the head and make sure that the edges of the "U" are symmetrical either side of the shank. (Diagrams 6.17, 6.18 and 6.19).

One of the most effective bass bugs that has stood the test of time is the Gerbubble Bug invented in the 1920s by Tom Loving. It was one of the first bugs I made from balsa wood and caught many bass for me and my friends in the 1-to 2-pound range. In the 1970s along came Dave Whitlock's deer-hair version which is easier to make, casts well and has plenty of movement in the water. Just for fun I decided to make a "Hairy" Gerbubble Bug. It has proved just as successful as the original and that of Whitlock's, but in some ways the divided tails of fox fur give it more appeal to the fish. Tie it in your favourite colours and try it out.

⇜ Hairy Black Forktailed Gerbubble Bug ⇝

Hook: TMC 8089, Mustad 80300BR or Daiichi 2720 sizes 2/0-10.

Thread: Black 4/0 or 6/0.

Tail: Dyed black fox fur (long fibred) or dyed-black goat hair.

Collar: Dyed black fox fur.

Body side hackles: Preformed natural black-tipped grey fox tail.

Underbody: Two lengths of 50-pound monofilament tied on either side of the hook shank to widen the body.

Body: Black stacked over grey deer body hair.

Head: Dyed red deer body hair.

Weed guard: "U"-shaped stainless steel wire.

Tying the Hairy Black Forktailed Gerbubble Bug
(Diagrams 6.20 and 6.20a)

Step 1: Place the hook in the vise's jaws.

Step 2: Form a firm thread base over the shank from eye to bend of the hook.

Step 3: By using Step 2(a) of formation of "hair hackle" legs, form the hind legs of black fox fur with fibre length equal to 1 1/2 times the length of the hook's shank.

Step 4: Construct a hair-hackle collar of black fox fur with fibre length 3/4 of the shank's length. Wrap it forward to opposite the hook point, and tie off.

Step 5: Bind in the 2 lengths of 50-pound monofilament on either side of the hook shank. Cut their front ends off an eye's length from the eye. Tie in, half hitch and varnish.

Step 6: Now tie in the Matuka-style body hackles on either side of the monofilament lengths. You now have a wide base on which to build the deer-hair body.

Step 7: Stack black over grey deer hair to 1/4 of the shank's length from the eye of the hook and tie off.

Step 8: Trim the deer-hair body into a rectangular shape with its height 1/2 its width, and 2/3 of its height above the shank.

Step 9: Bring the preformed body hackles forward level

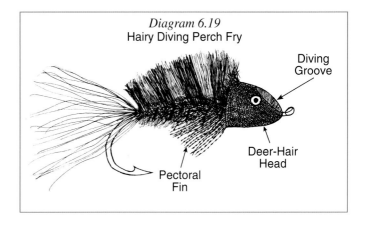

Diagram 6.19
Hairy Diving Perch Fry

Diving
Groove

Deer-Hair
Head

Pectoral
Fin

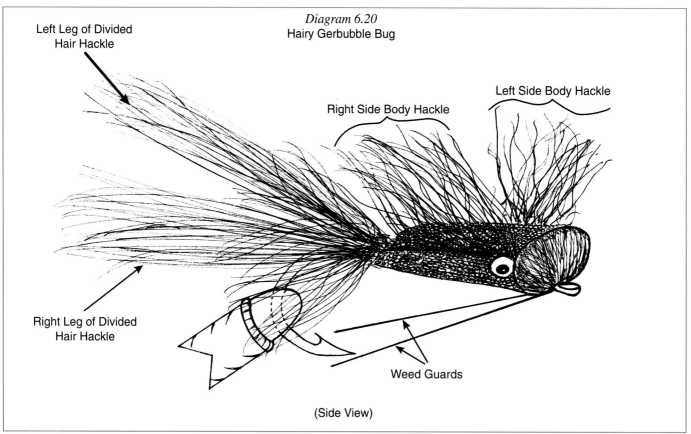

Diagram 6.20
Hairy Gerbubble Bug

Left Leg of Divided
Hair Hackle

Right Side Body Hackle

Left Side Body Hackle

Right Leg of Divided
Hair Hackle

Weed Guards

(Side View)

with shank. Pull them well into the sides of the body, tie in, cut off hackle butts and half hitch. Make sure the front 1/4 of the shank has smooth bindings on which to form the bug's head.

Step 10: Spin the red deer hair for the head of the bug. Trim the head to the same shape as the body.

Step 11: Varnish the bottom and front of the head. If you wish to animate the bug, add hollow plastic doll's eyes to each side of the head.

Step 12: Complete the bug with the addition of the weed guard.

There are many bass bugs that can be made into Hairys. I hope those listed above will inspire you to transform others into bugs made entirely of hair. What about "Hairy" Whistlers for a start?

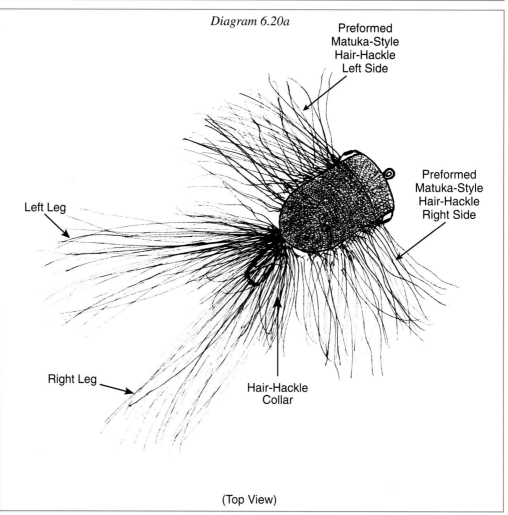

Diagram 6.20a

Preformed
Matuka-Style
Hair-Hackle
Left Side

Preformed
Matuka-Style
Hair-Hackle
Right Side

Left Leg

Right Leg

Hair-Hackle
Collar

(Top View)

Hair-Hackle Tying Techniques & Fly Patterns

Chapter 7

Hairy Fly and Bug Patterns

Trout
Pupae

Hairy Crane Fly Pupa

Hook: TMC2487, Partridge K4A, Mustad 80250BR, Daiichi 1130 sizes 10-18 wtd.
Thread: Yellow 6/0 or 8/0.
Weight: Copper or lead wire.
Ribbing: Gold wire.

Body: Cream underfur from woodchuck.
Head: Ginger dubbing.

Hairy Cream Pupa

Hook: TMC2487, Partridge K4A, Mustad 80250BR, Daiichi 1130 sizes 10-18 wtd.
Thread: Yellow 6/0 or 8/0.
Weight: Copper or lead wire.
Ribbing: Gold wire.

Body: Cream underfur from a woodchuck.
Head: Black Flashabou dubbing for general pattern.

Hairy Green Pupa

Hook: TMC 2487, Partridge K4A, Mustad 80250BR, Daiichi 1130 sizes 10-18 wtd.
Thread: Olive or yellow 6/0 or 8/0.
Weight: Copper or lead wire.
Ribbing: Gold wire.

Body: Dyed olive fur.
Head: Back Flashabou dubbing.

Hairy Hare's Ear Pupa

Hook: TMC 2487, Partridge K4A, Mustad 80250BR, Daiichi 1130 sizes 10-18 wtd.
Thread: Yellow 6/0 or 8/0.
Weight: Copper or lead wire.
Ribbing: Gold wire.

Body: Natural brown squirrel dubbing.
Head: Brown dubbing.

Hairy Blood Worm

Hook: TMC 400T, Partridge YK4ST sizes 10-14 wtd.
Thread: Red 6/0 or 8/0.
Weight: Copper wire tied over the middle 1/4 of the shank.
Tail: A mixture of hot orange and red woodchuck underfur.

Ribbing: Fluorescent orange floss.
Body: Dyed-red woodchuck underfur dubbing.
Thorax: Dyed-red woodchuck fur with guard hairs left in.
Head: Black dubbing well pricked out.

Hairy Brown Caddis Larva

Hook: TMC 200R, Mustad 89950BR, Daiichi 1270 sizes 8-16 wtd.
Thread: Black or tan 6/0 or 8/0.
Weight: Copper or lead wire.
Ribbing: Gold wire.
Body: Ginger dubbing.
Thorax: Fiery brown dubbing.

Hackle: Brown squirrel tail hairs.
Head: Black fur dubbing or black Angel Hair dubbing.

Hairy Olive Caddis Larva

Hook: TMC 200R, Mustad 89950BR, Daiichi 1270 sizes 8-16 wtd.
Thread: Yellow, olive or black 6/0 or 8/0.
Weight: Copper or lead wire.
Ribbing: Copper or gold wire.
Body: Medium, olive dubbing.

Thorax: Dark olive squirrel or rabbit fur dubbing.
Hackle: Dyed-olive squirrel tail hairs.
Head: Black fur dubbing or black Angel Hair dubbing.

Hairy Green Caddis Larva

Hook: TMC 200R, Mustad 8995BR, Daiichi 1270 sizes 8-18 wtd.
Thread: Green or olive 6/0 or 8/0.
Weight: Copper or lead wire.
Ribbing: Gold wire.
Body: Green dubbing.
Thorax: Ginger dubbing.

Hackle: Ginger or brown squirrel tail
Head: Black fur dubbing.

Hairy Hare's Ear Larva

Hook: TMC 200R, Mustad 8995BR, Daiichi 1270 sizes 8-18 wtd.
Thread: Yellow or cream 6/0 or 8/0.
Weight: Copper or lead wire.
Ribbing: Gold oval tinsel.
Body: Hare's ear or natural brown squirrel dubbing.

Thorax: Hare's ear or natural brown squirrel dubbing.
Hackle: Guard hairs from wild rabbit.
Head: Ginger dubbing.

Hairy Red-Eyed Blue-Winged Olive Nymph

Hook: TMC 5263, Mustad 9672, Daiichi 1720 sizes 8-14 wtd.
Thread: Cream or yellow 6/0 or 8/0.
Eyes: Nylon mono nymph eyes painted red.
Weight: Copper or lead wire.
Tail: Red fox squirrel body guard hairs.
Ribbing: Brown thread.
Body: Medium olive rabbit fur dubbing.

Underwing: Light grey fur with guard hairs.
Thorax: Medium olive rabbit fur dubbing.
Over wing: Dark grey fur with guard hairs.
Hackle: Brown guard hairs from grey squirrel pelt.
Head: Brown dubbing.

Nymphs

Hairy Red-Eyed Damsel Nymph

Hook: TMC 5263, Mustad 9672, Daiichi 1720 sizes 8-14 wtd.
Thread: Black, green or olive 6/0 or 8/0.
Eyes: Nylon mono nymph eyes painted red.
Weight: Copper or lead wire.
Tail: Olive arctic fox fur.

Ribbing: Olive tinsel thread.
Body: Olive rabbit dubbing (thin).
Underwing: Olive fur with guard hairs.
Thorax: Olive dubbing well pricked out.
Overwing: Grey fur with guard hairs.
Hackle: Olive squirrel tail.
Head: Black or brown dubbing.

Hairy Red-Eyed Fiery Brown Nymph

Hook: TMC 5263, Mustad 9672, Daiichi 1720 sizes 8-14 wtd.
Thread: Red or orange 6/0 or 8/0.
Eyes: Nylon mono nymph eyes painted red.
Weight: Copper or lead wire.
Tail: Fox squirrel tail dyed fiery brown.
Ribbing: Gold oval tinsel.
Body: Fiery brown fur dubbing (thin).

Underwing: Ginger fur with guard hairs.
Thorax: Dark brown fur dubbing.
Over wing: Fiery brown fur with guard hairs.
Hackle: Fox squirrel tail dyed fiery brown.
Head: Black or brown dubbing.

Hairy Red-Eyed Gold Ribbed Hare's Ear Nymph

Hook: TMC 5263, Mustad 9672, Daiichi 1720 sizes 8-14 wtd.
Thread: Yellow 6/0 or 8/0.
Weight: Copper or lead wire.
Tail: Light natural wild rabbit fur.
Ribbing: Gold oval tinsel.
Body: Hare's ear dubbing.
Underwing: Light natural wild rabbit fur.
Thorax: Well pricked out hare's ear dubbing.
Overwing: Dark natural wild rabbit fur.
Hackle: Light natural wild rabbit guard hairs.
Head: Ginger fur dubbing.

Hairy Red-Eyed MacMonty Nymph

Hook: TMC 5268, Mustad 9672, Daiichi 1720 sizes 8-14 wtd.
Thread: Black 6/0 or 8/0.
Eyes: Nylon mono nymph eyes painted red.
Weight: Copper or lead wire.
Tail: Black squirrel tail.
Body: Black fur dubbing.
Under wing: Black fur.
Thorax: Yellow dubbing.
Over wing: Black fur.
Hackle: Black squirrel tail.
Head: Fluorescent green dubbing.

Hackle Flies

Hairy Red-Eyed Mayfly Nymph

Hook: TMC 5268, Mustad 9672, Daiichi 1720 sizes 8-14 wtd.
Thread: Cream or yellow 6/0 or 8/0.
Eyes: Nylon mono nymph eyes painted red.
Weight: Copper or lead wire.
Tail: Squirrel tail dyed brown
Ribbing: Brown thread.
Body: Cream woodchuck underfur dubbing.
Underwing: Ginger fur.
Thorax: Cream woodchuck underfur.
Over wing: Brown fur.
Hackle: Brown squirrel tail.
Head: Dark brown dubbing.

Hairy Black And Peacock Spider

Hook: TMC 921, Mustad 94838, Daiichi 1310 sizes 8-14.
Thread: Black 6/0 or 8/0.
Body: Bronze peacock herl.
Hackle: Soft black hair.

Hairy Black Pennell

Hook: TMC 921, Mustad 94838, Daiichi 1310 sizes 8-14.
Thread: Black 6/0 or 8/0.
Tag: Flat silver tinsel.
Tail: Black tipped woodchuck guard hairs dyed orange.
Ribbing: Silver wire.

Body: Black dubbing.
Hackle: Soft black hair.

Hairy Brown Squirrel Peacock

Hook: TMC 921, Mustad 94838, Daiichi 1310 sizes 8-14.
Thread: Black 6/0 or 8/0.
Tail: Dyed red squirrel tail "hair hackle".
Body: Bronze peacock herl.
Hackle: Natural red squirrel tail.

Hairy Black Spider

Hook: TMC 921, Mustad 94838, Daiichi 1310 sizes 8-14.
Thread: Black 6/0 or 8/0.
Tag: Flat silver tinsel.
Body: Black tying thread or black floss.
Hackle: Soft black hair.

Hairy Greenwell Spider

Hook: TMC 921, Mustad 94838, Daiichi 1310 sizes 8-14.
Thread: Yellow 6/0 or 8/0.
Tail: Short yellow Antron wool "hair hackle".
Ribbing: Gold wire.
Body: Well-waxed yellow tying thread.

Hackle: Grey squirrel dyed ginger.

Hairy Grey Fox Peacock

Hook: TMC 921, Mustad 94838,
Daiichi 1310 sizes 8-14.
Tail: Dyed red short squirrel tail.
Body: Bronze peacock herl.
Hackle: Grey fox guard hairs.

Hairy March Brown Spider

Hook: TMC 921, Mustad 94838, Daiichi
1310 sizes 8-14.
Thread: Yellow or orange 6/0 or 8/0
Tail: Natural rabbit guard hairs or
none.
Ribbing: Fine flat gold tinsel.
Body: Hare's ear dubbing.

Hackle: Speckled brown fox squirrel
guard hair.

Hairy Iron Blue Dun

Hook: TMC 921, Mustad 94838,
Daiichi 1310 sizes 8 -14.
Thread: Red 6/0 or 8/0.
Tail: Honey dun dyed squirrel.
Body: Dubbed dark grey fur showing
red tying thread at tail.
Hackle: Honey dun dyed squirrel.

Hairy Orange Fish Hawk

Hook: TMC 921, Mustad 94838,
Daiichi 1310 sizes 8-14.
Thread: Black 6/0 or 8/0.
Tag: Flat gold tinsel.
Ribbing: Flat gold tinsel.
Body: Orange floss silk.

Hackle: Black based, white-tipped
woodchuck fur.

Hairy Pheasant Tail

Hook: TMC 921, Mustad 94838, Daiichi 1310 sizes 8-16.
Thread: Olive or dark green 6/0 or 8/0.
Tail: Fox squirrel tail dyed fiery brown.
Ribbing: Fine copper wire
Body: Long cock pheasant tail fibres.

Hackle: Speckled fox squirrel guard hairs.

Hairy Squirrel and Orange

Hook: TMC 921, Mustad 94838, Daiichi 1310 sizes 10-16.
Thread: Orange 6/0 or 8/0.
Tag: Flat gold tinsel.
Body: Orange floss silk and red dubbing.

Hackle: Combined mixture of long guard hairs and short underfur from fox squirrel skin.

Palmers

Hairy Squirrel and Green

Hook: TMC 921, Mustad 94838, Daiichi 1310 sizes 10 -16.
Thread: Green 6/0 or 8/0.
Tag: Flat silver tinsel.
Body: Thin green dubbing.

Hackle: Combined mixture of long guard hairs and short underfur from grey squirrel skin.

Hairy Bibio

Hook: TMC 3769, Partridge L2A, Mustad 3906B sizes 8-14.
Thread: Black 6/0 or 8/0.
Tag: Flat silver tinsel.
Ribbing: Silver wire incorporated into body hackle.

Body: In 3 equal parts. Front and rear black dubbing, middle red dubbing.
Body hackle: Preformed black squirrel tail.
Head hackle: Soft black hair.

Hairy Blue Zulu

Hook: TMC 3769, Partridge L2A, Mustad 3906B sizes 8-14.
Thread: Black 6/0 or 8/0.
Tail: Red wool.
Ribbing: Flat silver tinsel.
Body: Black fur dubbing.

Body hackle: Preformed black squirrel tail.
Head hackle: Dyed-blue hair.

Hairy Kate McLaren

Hook: TMC 3769, Partridge L2A, Mustad 3906B sizes 8-14.
Thread: Black 6/0 or 8/0.
Tail: Gold Antron wool.
Ribbing: Silver oval or wire.
Body hackle: Preformed black squirrel.

Head hackle: Longish ginger hair.

Hairy Doobry

Hook: TMC3769, Partridge L2A, Mustad 3906B sizes 8-14.
Thread: Black 6/0 or 8/0.
Tail: Fluorescent fire-red Antron wool.
Ribbing: Fine gold oval or in small sizes gold wire.
Body: Flat gold tinsel.

Body hackle: Preformed black squirrel tail.
Head hackle: Dyed hot orange followed black soft hair.

Hairy March Brown

Hook: TMC 3769, Partridge L2A, Mustad 3906B sizes 8-14.
Thread: Yellow 6/0 or 8/0.
Ribbing: Gold oval or wire.
Body: A mixture of 80% hare's ear and 20% yellow fur dubbing.
Body hackle: Preformed ginger hair.

Head hackle: Longish speckled fox squirrel guard hairs fairly full.

Hair-Hackle Tying Techniques & Fly Patterns

Hairy Pearly Wickhams

Hook: TMC 3769, Partridge L2A, Mustad 3906B sizes 8-14.
Thread: Black 6/0 or 8/0.
Tail: Ginger hair.
Ribbing: Silver wire.
Body: Flat pearl Mylar tinsel.

Body hackle: Preformed dark ginger or brown hair.
Head hackle: Dyed grey hair.

Hairy Black Woolly Bugger

Hook: TMC 5263, Mustad 9672, Daiichi 1720 sizes 4-12.
Thread: Black 6/0 or 8/0.
Tail: Black arctic fox fur with a few strands of black crystal hair mixed in.
Body: Black rabbit fur dubbing.

Body and head hackle: Preformed black arctic fox tail hair.

Hairy Soldier Palmer

Hook: TMC 3769, Partridge L2A, Mustad 3906B sizes 8-14
Thread: Red 6/0 or 8/0.
Tail: Red wool.
Ribbing: Oval gold tinsel.
Body: Red fur dubbing.
Body hackle: Preformed red hair.

Head hackle: Red hair.

Hairy Brown Woolly Bugger

Hook: TMC 5263, Mustad 9672, Daiichi 1720 sizes 4-12.
Thread: Black or brown 6/0 or 8/0.
Tail: Dyed brown fox fur with a few strands of brown crystal hair mixed in.
Body: Brown rabbit dubbing.

Body and head hackle: Preformed dyed brown fox tail hair.

Hairy Olive Woolly Bugger

Hook: TMC 5263, Mustad 9672, Daiichi 1720 sizes 4-12.
Thread: Olive or green 6/0 or 8/0.
Tail: Dyed olive fox fur with a few strands of olive crystal hair mixed in.
Body: Olive rabbit dubbing.

Body and head hackle: Preformed dyed-olive grey fox tail hairs.

Hairy Black Woolly Worm

Hook: TMC 5263, Mustad 9672, Daiichi 1720 sizes 4-12.
Thread: Black 6/0 or 8/0.
Tail: Red hair (dyed).
Body: Black rabbit dubbing.
Hackle: Preformed well-marked grey fox hair palmered over the body.

Woolly Worms

Hairy All Black Woolly Worm

Hook: TMC 5263, Mustad 9672, Daiichi 1720 sizes 4-12.
Thread: Black 6/0 or 8/0.
Tail: Dyed red hair.
Body: Black rabbit dubbing.
Hackle: Preformed black squirrel tail hairs palmered over the body.

Hairy Olive/Black Woolly Worm

Hook: TMC 5263, Mustad 9672, Daiichi 1720 sizes 4-12.
Thread: Olive 6/0 or 8/0.
Tail: Red hair (dyed).
Body: Olive rabbit dubbing.
Hackle: Preformed black squirrel tail hairs palmered over the body.

Hairy Yellow/Badger Woolly Worm

Hook: TMC 5263, Mustad 9672, Daiichi 1720 sizes 4-12.
Thread: Yellow 6/0 or 8/0.
Tail: Red hair (dyed).
Body: Yellow rabbit dubbing.

Hackle: Preformed white-tipped grey squirrel tail hairs palmered over the body.

Hairy Bibio Bomber

Hook: Partridge YL2A, Sprite International sizes 8-14. TMC 102Y sizes 9-15.
Thread: Black 6/0 or 8/0.
Tag: Flat silver tinsel.
Head Hackle: Dyed-black squirrel tail.

Ribbing: Built-in wire stem of preformed hackle.
Body: Front and rear thirds, black deer hair; middle third, red deer hair.
Body hackle: Preformed black squirrel tail hair.

Trout Bombers

Hairy Aberdeen Angus Bomber

Hook: Partridge YL2A, Sprite International sizes 8-14, TMC 102 Y sizes 9-15.
Thread: Yellow 6/0 or 8/0.
Tag: Gold oval tinsel or gold wire.
Tail: Ginger hair.

Ribbing: Built-in wire stem of preformed hackle.
Body: Rear half, yellow deer hair. Front half, red deer hair.
Body hackle: Preformed ginger or brown hair.
Head hackle: Speckled hair from base of fox squirrel.

Hairy Blue Zulu Bomber

Hook: Partridge YL2A, Sprite International sizes 8-14, TMC 102Y sizes 9-15.
Thread: Black 6/0 or 8/0.
Tag: Flat silver tinsel.
Tail: Red wool.

Ribbing: Built-in wire stem of preformed hackle.
Body: Black deer body hair.
Body hackle: Preformed black squirrel tail hair.
Head hackle: Dyed-blue hair.

Hairy Clan Chief Bomber

Hook: Partridge YL2A, Sprite International sizes 8-14, TMC 102Y sizes 9-15.

Thread: Black 6/0 or 8/0.

Tag: Flat silver tinsel.

Tail: Red over yellow fluorescent Antron wool.

Ribbing: Built-in stem of preformed hackle.

Body: Black deer body hair.

Body hackle: Preformed black & dyed red squirrel tail hair.

Head hackle: Softer black hair.

Hairy Invicta Bomber

Hook: Partridge YL2A, Sprite International sizes 8-14, TMC 102Y sizes 9-15.

Thread: Yellow 6/0 or 8/0.

Tag: Flat gold tinsel.

Tail: Yellow Antron wool.

Ribbing: Built-in stem of preformed hackle.

Body: Yellow or golden olive deer body hair.

Body hackle: Preformed of ginger or brown hair.

Head hackle: Brown speckled hair from fox squirrel tail, plus fibres of blue jay.

Hairy Claret Squirrel Bomber

Hook: Partridge YL2A, Sprite International sizes 8-14. TMC 102Y sizes 9-15.

Thread: Red or black 6/0 or 8/0.

Tag: Flat gold tinsel.

Tail: Black-tipped woodchuck guard hairs dyed orange.

Ribbing: Built-in stem of preformed hackle.

Body: Claret deer body hair.

Body hackle: Mixed red and black squirrel tail hair.

Head hackle: Speckled brown hair from the base of a fox squirrel.

Hairy Ross Bomber

Hook: Partridge YL2A, Sprite International sizes 8-14, TMC 102Y sizes 9-15.

Thread: Red 6/0 or 8/0.

Tag: Flat silver tinsel.

Tail: Black-tipped woodchuck guard hairs dyed orange.

Ribbing: Built-in stem of preformed hackle.

Body: Rear half, white deer hair. Front half, red deer hair.

Body hackle: Preformed of silver Angel Hair followed by black hair.

Head hackle: Speckled grey squirrel hair from base of the tail.

Hairy Squirrel Blue and Grey Bomber

Hook: Partridge YL2A, Sprite International sizes 8-14, TMC 102Y sizes 9-15.
Thread: Black 6/0 or 8/0.
Tag: Flat silver tinsel.
Tail: Black-tipped woodchuck guard hairs dyed orange.

Ribbing: Built-in stem of preformed hackle.
Body: Dyed grey deer body hair.
Body hackle: Dyed-blue hair.
Head hackle: Speckled grey squirrel hair from base of tail.

Hairy Black Matuka

Hook: TMC 5263, Partridge D4 A, Daiichi 1720 or 2220, Mustad 9672 or 79580 sizes 4-12.
Thread: Black 6/0 or 8/0.
Tag: Flat or oval silver tinsel.
Tail: Black squirrel tail hairs.
Ribbings: Oval silver tinsel and clear monofilament.

Body: Rear 3/4, black dubbing, front 1/4, red dubbing.
Matuka hackle: Preformed black squirrel tail hairs.
Head hackle: Dyed-black squirrel tail hairs.

Hairy Zulu Bomber

Hook: Partridge YL2A, Sprite International sizes 8-14, TMC 102 Y sizes 9-15.
Thread: Black 6/0 or 8/0.
Tag: Flat silver tinsel.
Tail: Red wool.

Ribbing: Built-in stem of preformed hackle.
Body: Black deer body hair.
Body hackle: Black squirrel tail hair.
Head hackle: Black squirrel tail hair.

Hairy Olive Matuka

Hook: TMC 5263, Partridge D4A, Daiichi 1720 or 2220, Mustad 9672 or 79580 sizes 4-12.
Thread: Olive or green 6/0 or 8/0.
Tag: Flat or oval gold tinsel.
Tail: Olive-dyed grey squirrel tail hairs.

Ribbings: Oval gold tinsel and clear monofilament.
Body: Rear 3/4, olive dubbing, front 1/4, red dubbing.
Matuka hackle: Olive-dyed grey squirrel tail hairs.
Head hackle: Olive-dyed grey squirrel tail hairs.

Hairy Purple Matuka

Hook: TMC 5263, Partridge D4A, Daiichi 1720 or 2220, Mustad 9672 or 79580 sizes 4-12.
Thread: Black 6/0 or 8/0.
Tag: Flat or oval silver tinsel.
Tail: Purple-dyed grey squirrel tail hairs.

Ribbings: Oval silver tinsel and clear monofilament.
Body: Rear 3/4, purple dubbing, front 1/4 red dubbing.
Matuka hackle: Purple-dyed grey squirrel tail hairs.
Head hackle: Purple-dyed grey squirrel tail hairs.

Hairy Green Sedge

Hook: Partridge 01 sizes 10-16, TMC 5212 sizes 4-10.
Thread: Green or black 6/0 or 8/0.
Tail: A bunch of natural brown deer hair.
Ribbing: Clear monofilament.

Wing: Preformed Matuka-style hackle of natural brown deer hair.
Body: Dubbing brush of green deer body hair, trimmed to shape.
Hackle: Ginger hair.
Antennae: Two moose mane hairs.

Sedges

Hairy Black Sedge

Hook: Partridge 01 sizes 10-16, TMC 5212 sizes 4-10.
Thread: Black 6/0 or 8/0.
Tail: A bunch of natural darkest brown deer hair.
Ribbing: Clear monofilament.

Wing: Preformed Matuka-style hackle of natural darkest brown deer hair.
Body: Dubbing brush of black deer hair, trimmed to shape.
Hackle: Black hair.
Antennae: Two moose mane hairs.

Hairy Orange Sedge

Hook: Partridge 01 sizes 10-16, TMC 5212 sizes 4-10.
Thread: Orange or yellow 6/0 or 8/0.
Tail: A bunch of natural brown deer hair.
Ribbing: Clear monofilament.

Wing: Preformed Matuka-style hackle of natural brown deer hair.
Body: Dubbing brush of orange deer body hair.
Hackle: Brown or ginger hair.
Antennae: Two moose mane hairs.

Hairy Black Gnat Emerger

Hook: TMC 5212, Partridge H1A, Mustad 94831, Daiichi 1280 sizes 10-16.
Thread: Black 6/0 or 8/0.
Shuck: Grey Antron wool.
Tail: Black hair.
Ribbing: Black floss or tying thread.

Body: Black dubbing.
Wings: Grey deer body hair.
Thorax: Black dubbing.
Hackle: Black hair.

Hairy March Brown Emerger

Hook: TMC 5212, Partridge H1A, Mustad 94831, Daiichi 1280 sizes 10-16.
Thread: Yellow 6/0 or 8/0.
Shuck: Olive Antron wool.
Tail: Wild rabbit fur.
Ribbing: Gold wire.

Body: Brown speckled squirrel fur dubbing.
Wings: Dyed-brown deer body hair.
Thorax: Brown speckled squirrel fur dubbing.
Hackle: Fox squirrel guard

Hairy Blue Dun Emerger

Hook: TMC 5212, Partridge H1A, Mustad 94831, Daiichi 1280 sizes 10-16.
Thread: Black or grey 6/0 or 8/0.
Shuck: Grey Antron wool.
Tail: Dyed grey woodchuck guard hairs.

Ribbing: Brown thread.
Body: Blue dun dubbing.
Wings: Grey deer body hair.
Thorax: Blue dun dubbing.
Hackle: Dyed-natural woodchuck guard hairs.

Hairy Olive Dun Emerger

Hook: TMC 5212, Partridge H1A, Mustad 94831, Daiichi 1280 sizes 10-16.
Thread: Green or olive 6/0 or 8/0.
Shuck: Medium olive Antron wool.
Tail: Olive fur.
Ribbing: Olive or gold around thread.

Body: Olive fur dubbing.
Wings: Dyed-olive deer body hair.
Thorax: Olive fur dubbing.
Hackle: Dyed-olive grey squirrel tail hairs.

Hairy Yellow May Emerger

Hook: TMC 5212, Partridge H1A, Mustad 94831, Daiichi 1280 sizes 10-16.
Thread: Yellow 6/0 or 8/0.
Shuck: Fluorescent yellow Antron wool.
Tail: Fine yellow hair.
Ribbing: Gold wire.
Body: Bright yellow fur dubbing.
Wings: Dyed golden olive deer body hair.
Thorax: Yellow fur dubbing.
Hackle: Ginger hair.

Hairy Claret Midge Emerger

Hook: Partridge YK2B, TMC 2487, Daiichi 1150 sizes 10-16.
Thread: Red 6/0 or 8/0.
Shuck: Pink Antron wool.
Tail: White Antron wool.
Ribbing: Gold wire.
Body: Claret dubbing.
Wing buds: Olive over orange Antron wool.
Thorax: Claret fur dubbing.
Hackle: Black hair.
Gills: White Antron wool.

Midge Emergers

Hairy Black Midge Emerger

Hook: Partridge YK2B, TMC 2487, Daiichi 1150 sizes 10-16.
Thread: Black 6/0 or 8/0.
Shuck: Grey Antron wool.
Tail: White Antron wool.
Ribbing: Silver wire.
Body: Black dubbing.
Wing buds: Olive over orange Antron wool.
Thorax: Black fur dubbing.
Hackle: Fine black hair.
Gills: White Antron wool.

Hairy Golden Olive Midge Emerger

Hook: Partridge YK2B, TMC 2487, Daiichi 1150 sizes 10-16.
Thread: Yellow 6/0 or 8/0.
Shuck: Fluorescent green Antron wool.
Tail: White Antron wool.
Ribbing: Gold wire.
Body: Golden olive dubbing.
Wing buds: Olive over orange Antron wool.
Thorax: Olive fur dubbing.
Hackle: Ginger or golden olive hairs.
Gills: White Antron wool.

Hairy Olive Midge Emerger

Hook: Partridge YK2B, TMC 2487, Daiichi 1150 sizes 10-16.
Thread: Yellow or olive 6/0 or 8/0.
Shuck: Medium olive Antron wool.
Tail: White Antron wool.
Ribbing: Gold wire.
Body: Medium olive fur dubbing.

Wing buds: Olive over orange Antron wool.
Thorax: Green olive fur dubbing.
Hackle: Olive hair.
Gills: White Antron wool.

Hairy Olive Shrimp

Hook: Partridge YK2B, Daiichi 1150 sizes 10-16 wtd.
Thread: Cream or olive 6/0 or 8/0.
Weight: Copper or lead wire.
Antennae: Two strands of pearl crystal hair.
Tail hackle: Dyed-olive woodchuck fur.

Eyes: Black mono nymph eyes.
Legs: Preformed hackle of olive woodchuck fur.
Ribbing: Clear monofilament.
Body: Olive woodchuck fur dubbing.
Shell back: Olive grey squirrel tail hairs.

Freshwater Shrimp

Hairy Grey Shrimp

Hook: Partridge YK2B, Daiichi 1150 sizes 10-16 wtd.
Thread: Black 6/0 or 8/0.
Weight: Copper or lead wire.
Antennae: Two strands of pearl crystal hair.
Tail hackle: Speckled grey squirrel fur.

Eyes: Mono nymph eyes painted black.
Legs: Preformed hackle of grey woodchuck fur.
Ribbing: Clear monofilament.
Body: Grey fur dubbing.
Shell back: Grey squirrel tail hairs, varnished.

Hairy Tan Shrimp

Hook: Partridge YK2B, Daiichi 1150 sizes 10-16 wtd.
Thread: Cream 6/0 or 8/0.
Weight: Copper or lead wire.
Antennae: Two strands of pearl crystal hair.
Tail hackle: Ginger fur.

Eyes: Black mono nymph eyes.
Legs: Preformed hackle of ginger or tan fur.
Ribbing: Clear monofilament.
Body: Ginger fur dubbing.
Shell back: Squirrel tail hairs dyed fiery brown.

Fry or Baitfish

Salmon, Sea Trout and Steelhead Flies

(*All patterns marked with an asterisk can be tied on trailer tandems.)

Hairy Black Leggie*

Hook: Singles: Partridge YL2A sizes 8-14.
Doubles: Partridge R2A sizes 10-16.
Thread: Black 6/0 or 8/0.
Tag: Flat silver tinsel.
Tail: Black squirrel tail hairs.
Ribbing: Silver oval or wire.

Palmer hackle: Preformed black hair, Spey style.
Body: Black fur dubbing.
Head hackle No. 1: Fine black bucktail.
Head hackle No. 2: Blue jay.

Hairy Minnow

Hook: Partridge N, TMC 7989 sizes 4-12 wtd.
Weedless: Keel hook, Daiichi 1730 sizes 4-12 wtd.
Thread: Green or tan 6/0 or 8/0.
Weight: Lead or tungsten wire.
Tail: Black- or brown-tipped woodchuck guard hairs.
Back: Preformed Matuka hackle of olive rabbit fur.
Ribbing: Clear monofilament.

Body: Mixture of 40% olive, 60% cream dubbing fur.
Pectoral fins: Black-tipped wood chuck guard hairs.
Gills: Dyed-red rabbit fur dubbing.
Collar: Olive over grey deer hair.
Head: Olive stacked over grey deer hair trimmed to an oval fish-head shape with flat sides.
Eyes: Gold epoxy eyes.

Hairy Yellow Perch Fry

Hook: Partridge N, TMC 7989 sizes 4-12 wtd.
Weedless: Keel hook or Daiichi 1730 sizes 4-12 wtd.
Thread: Yellow or olive 4/0, 6/0 or 8/0.
Weight: Lead or tungsten wire.
Tail: Olive and sparse orange squirrel hair.
Ribbing: Clear monofilament.
Back: Preformed Matuka style hackle of 6 alternate bunches of black and olive rabbit fur.
Body: Mixture of 60% yellow and 40% fluorescent yellow fur well pricked out.

Pectoral fins: Orange squirrel tail hairs.
Gills: Red rabbit fur dubbing.
Collar: Olive over black deer body hair stacked over golden olive deer body hair.
Head: Olive and black deer body hair stacked over golden olive deer body hair, trimmed to an oval fish-head shape with flat sides.
Eyes: Plastic eyes.

Hairy Golden Olive Leggie*

Hook: Singles: Partridge YL2 A sizes 8-14. Doubles: Partridge R2A sizes 10-16.
Thread: Yellow 6/0 or 8/0.
Tag: Flat gold tinsel.
Tail: Golden olive hair.
Ribbing: Gold oval or wire.

Palmer hackle: Preformed ginger hair, Spey style.
Body: Golden olive fur dubbing.
Head hackle No. 1: Fine golden olive bucktail.
Head hackle No. 2: Blue jay.

Hairy Pearly Purple Leggie*

Hook: Singles: Partridge YL2A sizes 8-14.
Doubles: Partridge R2A sizes 10-16.
Thread: Black 6/0 or 8/0.
Tag: Flat silver tinsel.
Tail: Purple grey squirrel tail hairs.
Ribbing: Silver oval or wire.

Palmer hackle: Preformed grey squirrel tail, Spey style.
Body: Rear 1/2 flat pearl tinsel. Front 1/2 purple dubbing.
Head hackle No. 1: Fine purple bucktail.
Head hackle No. 2: Blue jay.

Hairy All Black Bumpadab

Hook: Partridge YL2A, TMC 5210 sizes 6-12.
Thread: Black 6/0 or 8/0.
Tag: Flat silver tinsel.
Tail: Black hair.
Ribbing: Silver oval tinsel or wire.

Palmer hackle: Preformed of black hair.
Body: Black fur dubbing.
Head hackle No. 1: Black hair.
Head hackle No. 2: Blue jay.

Hairy Silver Blue Leggie*

Hook: Singles: Partridge YL2A sizes 8-14.
Doubles: Partridge R2A sizes 10-16.
Thread: Black 6/0 or 8/0.
Tag: Flat silver tinsel.
Tail: Yellow Antron wool.
Ribbing: Silver wire.

Palmer hackle: Preformed blue hair, Spey style.
Body: Flat silver tinsel.
Head hackle No. 1: Grey fox tail, well marked.
Head hackle No. 2: Blue jay.

Hairy Bibio Bumpadab

Hook: Partridge YL2A, TMC 5210 sizes 6-12.
Thread: Black 6/0 or 8/0.
Tag: Flat silver tinsel.
Tail: None or black hair.
Ribbing: Silver oval tinsel or wire.

Palmer hackle: Preformed of black hair.
Body: Rear and front thirds black dubbing, centre third red or orange dubbing.
Head hackle No. 1: Black hair.
Head hackle No. 2: Blue jay.

Hairy Connemara Black Bumpadab

Hook: Partridge YL2A, TMC 5210 sizes 6-12.
Thread: Black 6/0 or 8/0.
Tag: Flat silver tinsel.
Tail: Fluorescent yellow Antron wool.
Ribbing: Silver oval tinsel or wire.

Palmer hackle: Preformed of black hair.
Body: Black fur dubbing.
Head hackle No. 1: Barred grey, brown, black hairs from a Russian black squirrel.
Head hackle No. 2: Blue jay.

Hairy Dunkeld Bumpadab*

Hook: Partridge YL2A, TMC 5210 sizes 6-12.
Thread: Yellow or orange 6/0 or 8/0.
Tag: Flat gold tinsel.
Tail: Yellow Antron wool fibres.
Ribbing: Gold wire.

Palmer hackle: Preformed orange hair.
Body: Flat gold tinsel
Head hackle No. 1: Natural barred black Russian squirrel.
Head hackle No. 2: Blue jay.

Hairy Claret Bumpadab

Hook: Partridge YL2A, TMC 5210 sizes 6-12.
Thread: Black or red 6/0 or 8/0.
Tag: Flat gold tinsel.
Tail: Dyed-orange black-tipped woodchuck hair.
Ribbing: Gold oval tinsel or wire.

Palmer hackle: Preformed of black hair.
Body: Claret dubbing.
Head hackle No. 1: Dyed claret hair.
Head hackle No. 2: Blue jay.

Hairy Fiery Brown Bumpadab

Hook: Partridge YL2A, TMC 5210 sizes 6-12.
Thread: Orange or brown 6/0 or 8/0.
Tag: Flat gold tinsel.
Tail: Red hair or Antron wool.
Ribbing: Gold wire.
Palmer hackle: Fiery brown hair.

Body: Fiery brown fur dubbing.
Head hackle No. 1: Red fox squirrel dyed fiery brown.
Head hackle No. 2: Blue jay.

Hairy Golden Olive Bumpadab

Hook: Partridge YL2A, TMC 5210 sizes 6-12.
Thread: Yellow 6/0 or 8/0.
Tag: Flat gold tinsel.
Tail: Yellow or fluorescent yellow Antron wool.
Ribbing: Gold wire.

Palmer hackle: Golden olive hair.
Body: Golden olive dubbing.
Head hackle No. 1: Grey squirrel tail dyed golden olive.
Head hackle No. 2: Blue jay.

Hairy Green Pete Bumpadab

Hook: Partridge YL2A, TMC 5210 sizes 6-12.
Thread: Green or black 6/0 or 8/0.
Tag: Flat gold tinsel.
Tail: Orange hair or fluorescent orange Antron wool.
Ribbing: Gold wire.

Palmer hackle: Green hair.
Body: Green fur dubbing.
Head hackle No. 1: Barred red fox squirrel tail.
Head hackle No. 2: Blue jay.

Hairy Gorbenmac Bumpadab*

Hook: Trailer tandem mounts.
Thread: Black or red 6/0.
Tag: Braided silver Mylar on treble hook.
Tail: Black tipped woodchuck hair dyed orange

Ribbing: Dubbing brush of bronze peacock
Palmer hackle: Ginger or brown hair.
Body: Yellow fur dubbing.
Head hackle No. 1: Speckled hair from dark fox squirrel tail.
Head hackle No. 2: Blue jay.

Hairy Invicta Bumpadab*

Hook: Partridge YL2A, TMC 5210 sizes 6-12.
Thread: Yellow 6/0 or 8/0.
Tag: Flat gold tinsel.
Tail: Fluorescent yellow Antron wool.
Ribbing: Gold wire.
Palmer hackle: Ginger or brown hair.

Body: Yellow fur dubbing.
Head hackle No. 1: Speckled hair from dark fox squirrel tail.
Head hackle No. 2: Blue jay.

Hairy Orkney Bumpadab

Hook: Partridge YL2A, TMC 5210 sizes 6-12.
Thread: Yellow 6/0 or 8/0.
Tag: Flat gold tinsel.
Tail: Fluorescent yellow Antron wool.
Ribbing: Gold wire.
Palmer hackle: Orange hair.

Body: Golden olive fur dubbing.
Head hackle No. 1: Grey squirrel tail dyed golden olive.
Head hackle No. 2: Blue jay.

Hairy Prince Charming Bumpadab*

Hook: Partridge YL2A, TMC 5210 sizes 6-12.
Thread: Black 6/0 or 8/0.
Tag: Flat silver tinsel.
Tail: Black-tipped woodchuck dyed orange.
Ribbing: Silver wire.

Palmer hackle: Speckled grey squirrel hair dyed blue.
Body: Rear and front thirds peacock herl. Middle third flat silver tinsel.
Head hackle No. 1: Grey squirrel tail dyed royal blue.
Head hackle No. 2: Blue jay.

Hairy Thunderer Bumpadab*

Hook: Partridge YL2A, TMC 5210 sizes 6-12.
Thread: Black 6/0 or 8/0.
Tag: Flat gold tinsel.
Tail: Fluorescent yellow Antron wool.
Ribbing: Gold wire.
Palmer hackle: Orange hair.

Body: Black fur dubbing.
Head hackle No. 1: Barred black or brown Russian squirrel hair.
Head hackle No. 2: Blue jay.

Hairy Silver Blue Bumpadab*

Hook: Partridge YL2A, TMC 5210 sizes 6-12.
Thread: Black 6/0 or 8/0.
Tag: Flat silver tinsel.
Tail: Fluorescent yellow Antron wool.
Ribbing: Silver wire.
Palmer hackle: Blue hair.

Body: Flat silver tinsel.
Head hackle No. 1: Grey squirrel tail hair.
Head hackle No 2: Blue jay.

Hair-Hackle Tying Techniques & Fly Patterns

Trailer Tandem Wake Flies

Hairy Night Muddler Black

Hook: Trailer tandem mount.
Thread: Black 4/0 or 6/0.
Treble hook body: Flat silver Mylar braid.
Treble hook hackle: Fluorescent yellow Antron wool.

Tail hackle: Black deer hair.
Body: Preformed hackle of black deer hair.

Hairy Night Muddler Yellow

Hook: Trailer tandem mount.
Thread: Black, red or yellow 4/0 or 6/0.
Treble hook body: Fluorescent green floss.
Tail: Yellow deer body hair.
Tail hackle: Black deer hair.

Body: Preformed of yellow deerbody hair.

Hairy Night Muddler Blue and White

Hook: Trailer tandem mount.
Thread: Black 4/0 or 6/0.
Treble hook body: Flat silver Mylar braid.
Treble hook hackle: Fluorescent yellow Antron wool.
Tail hackle: White deer hair.

Body: Preformed hackle: Rear 1/2 white deer hair.
Front 1/2 blue deer hair.

Low-Water Sea Trout Flies

Hairy Dunkeld

Hook: Partridge 01 sizes 6-14.
Thread: Black 6/0 or 8/0.
Tag: Gold oval tinsel
Tail: None.
Ribbing: Gold oval tinsel or wire.
Body: Flat gold tinsel.

Wing: Brown speckled squirrel tail hair over pearl crystal hair.
Hackle: Orange hair.

Hairy Gold Peter Ross

Hook: Partridge 01 sizes 6-14.
Thread: Black 6/0 or 8/0.
Tail: None.
Ribbing: Gold oval tinsel.
Body: Rear 1/2 flat gold tinsel. Front 1/2 red fur dubbing.
Wing: Grey speckled hair from the base of a grey squirrel's tail and 2 strands of pearl crystal hair.
Hackle: Black hair.

Hairy Silver Stoat Tail

Hook: Partridge 01 sizes 6-14.
Thread: Black 6/0 or 8/0.
Tag: Silver wire.
Tail: None.
Ribbing: Silver wire.
Body: Flat silver tinsel.
Wing: Black squirrel tail hair over pearl crystal hair.
Hackle: Black squirrel tail hair.

Salmon and Steelhead Flies
Hairy Salmon Flies

Hairy Silver Blue

Hook: Partridge 01 sizes 6-14.
Thread: Red 6/0 or 8/0.
Tag: Silver oval tinsel.
Tail: None.
Ribbing: Silver oval tinsel or wire.
Body: Flat silver tinsel.
Wing: Grey squirrel tail hair over pearl crystal hair.
Hackle: Blue hair.
Head: Varnish.

Hairy Black Bear Green Butt

Hook: Single: Partridge M, TMC 7999, Daiichi 2441 sizes 2-12.
Double: Partridge P sizes 2-12.
Thread: Black 6/0 or 8/0.
Tag: Silver oval or wire.
Butt: Fluorescent green floss.
Tail: Black hair.
Ribbing: Silver oval tinsel.
Body: Black fur dubbing.
Trailing hackle: Black squirrel or bear hair.
Front hackle: Black squirrel tail hair.

Hairy Blue Charm

Hook: Single: Partridge M, TMC 7999, Daiichi 2441 sizes 2-12.
Double: Partridge P sizes 2-12.
Thread: Black 6/0 or 8/0.
Tag: Silver tinsel and yellow floss.
Tail: Yellow Antron wool.
Ribbing: Silver oval tinsel.

Body: Black floss.
Trailing hackle: Grey squirrel tail hair.
Front hackle: Dyed blue hair.

Hairy Dunkeld

Hook: Partridge M, TMC 7999, Daiichi 2441 sizes 4-12.
Thread: Yellow or orange 6/0 or 8/0.
Tag: Flat or oval gold tinsel.
Tail: Yellow Antron wool under red Antron wool.
Butt: Black ostrich herl.

Body: Embossed gold braided Mylar tinsel.
Trailing hackle: Grey squirrel tail hairs dyed orange.
Front hackle: Hot orange hair.

Hairy Cain's Copper

Hook: Single: Partridge M, TMC 7999, Daiichi 2441 sizes 2-12.
Double: Partridge P sizes 2-12.
Thread: Orange 6/0 or 8/0.
Tag: Copper wire.
Tail: Dyed yellow hair or Antron wool.
Butt: Black ostrich herl.

Ribbing: Copper wire.
Body: Flat copper tinsel.
Trailing hackle: Dyed orange hair over which is 1 turn of grey squirrel tail hair.
Front hackle: Black squirrel tail hair.

Hairy Garry Dog

Hook: Single: Partridge M, TMC 7999, Daiichi 2441 sizes 2-12.
Double: Partridge P sizes 2-12.
Thread: Black 6/0 or 8/0.
Tag: Oval silver tinsel and yellow floss.
Tail: Dyed yellow hair or Antron wool.

Ribbing: Oval silver tinsel.
Body: Black floss.
Trailing hackle: Dyed yellow hair over dyed red hair.
Front hackle: Dyed blue hair.

Hairy Green Highlander

Hook Single: Partridge M, TMC 7999,
Daiichi 2441 sizes 2-12.
Double: Partridge P sizes 2-12.
Thread: Yellow 6/0 or 8/0.
Tag: Silver tinsel and yellow floss.
Tail: Yellow hair or Antron wool.
Ribbing: Sliver oval tinsel.

Body: Rear 1/2 yellow floss. Front 1/2
green highlander fur dubbing.
Trailing hackle: Grey squirrel dyed
green over grey squirrel dyed orange.
The orange squirrel palmered over
the front 1/2 of the body.
Front hackle: Dyed yellow hair.

Hairy Jock Scott

Hook: Single: Partridge M, TMC 7999,
Daiichi 2441 sizes 2-12.
Double: Partridge P sizes 2-12.
Thread: Yellow or black 6/0 or 8/0.
Tag: Silver tinsel and yellow floss.
Tail: Yellow Antron wool.
Butt: Black ostrich herl.
Ribbing: Oval silver tinsel.

Body: Rear 1/2 yellow floss. Front 1/2
black floss.
Trailing hackle: Natural red fox
squirrel over hair dyed: blue , over
red, over yellow.
Front hackle: Natural black-tipped
grey fox hair.

Hairy Hairy Mary

Hook: Single: Partridge M, TMC 7999,
Daiichi 2441 sizes 2-12.
Double: Partridge P sizes 2-12.
Thread: Black 6/0 or 8/0.
Tag: Gold tinsel.
Tail: Yellow Antron wool.
Ribbing: Oval gold tinsel.

Body: Black floss.
Trailing hackle: Natural red/brown
squirrel tail.
Front hackle: Dyed blue hair.

Hairy Munro Killer

Hook: Single: Partridge M, TMC 7999,
Daiichi 2441 sizes 2- 12.
Double: Partridge P sizes 2-12.
Thread: Black 6/0 or 8/0.
Tag: Gold tinsel.
Tail: Dyed orange hair.
Ribbing: Oval gold tinsel.

Body: Black floss.
Trailing hackle: Grey squirrel tail
dyed yellow.
Front hackle: Dyed orange hair
followed by grey squirrel tail dyed
kingfisher blue.

Hairy Silver Doctor

Hook: Single: Partridge M, TMC 7999, Daiichi 2441 sizes 2-12.
Double: Partridge P sizes 2-12.
Thread: Red or black 6/0 or 8/0.
Tag: Silver oval tinsel or wire
Tail: Yellow Antron wool.
Butt: Red wool.

Ribbing: Oval silver tinsel.
Body: Flat silver tinsel.
Trailing hackle: Blue over red over yellow dyed hair.
Front hackle: Blue hair.
Head: Red varnish.

Hairy Stoat's Tail

Hook: Single: Partridge M, TMC 7999, Daiichi 2441 sizes 2-12.
Double: Partridge P, sizes 2-12.
Thread: Black 6/0 or 8/0.
Tag: Silver wire.
Ribbing: Silver oval tinsel or wire.
Body: Black floss.

Trailing hackle: Black squirrel tail.
Front hackle: Black squirrel tail hair.

Hairy Salmon Shrimps

Hairy Silver Stoat's Tail

Hook: Single: Partridge M, TMC 7999, Daiichi 2441 sizes 2-12.
Double: Partridge P sizes 2-12.
Thread: Black 6/0 or 8/0.
Tag: Silver wire.
Tail: Yellow Antron wool.
Ribbing: Silver oval tinsel or wire.

Body: Flat silver tinsel.
Trailing hackle: Black squirrel tail hair.
Front hackle: Black squirrel tail hair.

Hairy Ally's Shrimp

Hook: Single: Partridge M, TMC 7999, Daiichi 2441 sizes 2-12.
Double: Partridge P sizes 4-12.
Thread: Red or orange 6/0 or 8/0.
Tag: Oval gold tinsel.
Antennae: Four strands of pearl crystal hair.
Tail: Orange hair.
Ribbing: Gold oval tinsel over whole body.

Body rear 1/2: Red floss or red fur dubbing.
Middle hackle: Grey squirrel tail hair.
Body front 1/2: Black floss or black fur dubbing.
Wings: Black-tipped woodchuck or grey fox dyed orange.
Front hackle: Orange hair.
Head: Red varnish.

Hairy Bann Special Shrimp

Hook: Single: Partridge M, TMC 7999, Daiichi 2441 sizes 2-12.
Double: Partridge P sizes 2-12.
Thread: Black or red 6/0 or 8/0.
Tag: Silver tinsel.
Tail: Grey squirrel tail dyed red.

Ribbing: Oval silver tinsel over whole body.
Rear 1/2 of body: Yellow fur dubbing.
Middle hackle: Orange hair.
Front 1/2 of body: Black fur dubbing.
Wing: Black-tipped grey fox hair.
Front hackle: Grey squirrel tail hairs.

Hairy Copper Shrimp

Hook: Single: Partridge M, TMC 7999, Daiichi 2441 sizes 2-12.
Double: Partridge P sizes 2-12.
Thread: Orange 6/0 or 8/0.
Tag: Copper wire.
Antennae: Pearl crystal.
Tail: Grey squirrel tail hair dyed orange.

Ribbing: Copper wire over whole body.
Body rear 1/2: Flat copper tinsel.
Middle hackle: Grey squirrel tail hair dyed orange.
Body front 1/2: Flat copper tinsel.
Wings: Dyed black squirrel tail hairs.
Front hackle: Grey squirrel tail hair dyed orange.

Hairy Curry's Red Shrimp

Hook: Single: Partridge M, TMC 7999, Daiichi 2441 sizes 2-12.
Double: Partridge P sizes 2-12.
Thread: Red 6/0 or 8/0.
Tag: Oval silver tinsel.
Tail: Grey squirrel tail hair dyed maroon.
Ribbing: Oval silver tinsel over whole body.
Body rear 1/2: Red floss or red fur dubbing.

Veiling: Red Antron wool (sparse).
Middle hackle: Grey squirrel tail hair.
Body front 1/2: Black floss or black fur dubbing.
Veiling: Red Antron wool (sparse).
Wings: Tent shaped of black-tipped grey fox hair.
Front hackle: Grey squirrel tail hair.
Head: Red varnish.

Hairy Faughan Shrimp

Hook: Single: Partridge M, TMC 7999, Daiichi 2441 sizes 2-12.
Double: Partridge P sizes 2-12.
Thread: Red 6/0 or 8/0.
Tag: Oval gold tinsel.
Tail: Grey squirrel tail hair dyed red.
Ribbing: Oval gold tinsel over whole body.

Body rear 1/2: Orange floss or fur dubbing.
Middle hackle: Orange hair.
Body front 1/2: Dark claret floss or fur dubbing
Wing: Black-tipped grey fox hair.
Front hackle: Grey squirrel tail hair dyed claret.

Hairy Foxford Shrimp

Hook: Single: Partridge M, TMC 7999, Daiichi 2441 sizes 2-12.
Double: Partridge P sizes 2-12.
Thread: Black 6/0 or 8/0.
Tag: Oval silver tinsel.
Tail: Grey squirrel tail hairs dyed red.
Ribbing: Oval silver tinsel over whole body.

Body rear 1/2: Black fur dubbing.
Middle hackle: Grey squirrel tail hairs.
Body front 1/2: Fiery brown fur dubbing.
Wings: Black-tipped grey fox hair.
Front hackle: Ginger hair.

Hairy Ness Shrimp

Hook: Single: Partridge M, TMC 7999, Daiichi 2441 sizes 2-12.
Double: Partridge P, sizes 2-12.
Thread: Black 6/0 or 8/0.
Tag: Silver oval tinsel.
Tail: Grey squirrel tail hair dyed red.

Ribbing: Oval silver tinsel over whole body.
Body rear 1/2: Orange fur dubbing.
Middle hackle: Orange hair.
Body front 1/2: Black fur dubbing.
Wings: Black-tipped grey fox hair.
Front hackle: Yellow followed by black hair.

Hairy Juner Shrimp

Hook: Single: Partridge M, TMC 7999, Daiichi 2441 sizes 2-12.
Double: Partridge P sizes 2-12.
Thread: Red 6/0 or 8/0.
Tag: Oval gold tinsel.
Tail: Grey squirrel tail hair dyed red.
Ribbing: Gold wire or gold oval tinsel.

Body rear 1/2: Red fur dubbing.
Middle hackle: Yellow hair.
Body front 1/2: Purple fur dubbing.
Wings: Black-tipped grey fox hair.
Front hackle: Grey squirrel tail hair dyed purple.

Hairy Wilkinson Shrimp

Hook: Single: Partridge M, TMC 7999, Daiichi 2441 sizes 2-12.
Double: Partridge P sizes 2-12.
Thread: Red 6/0 or 8/0.
Tag: Oval silver tinsel.
Tail: Grey squirrel tail hair dyed red.
Ribbing: Oval silver tinsel over whole body.

Body rear 1/2: Embossed silver tinsel or silver Mylar braid.
Middle hackle: Magenta hair.
Body front 1/2: Embossed silver tinsel or silver Mylar braid.
Wings: Black-tipped grey fox fur.
Front hackle: Light blue hair.

Hairy Yellow Ally's Shrimp

Hook: Single: Partridge M, TMC 7999, Daiichi 2441 sizes 2-12.
Double: Partridge P sizes 2-12.
Thread: Black 6/0 or 8/0.
Tag: Oval silver tinsel.
Antennae: Pearl crystal hair.
Tail: Yellow hair.
Ribbing: Silver oval tinsel over whole body.
Body rear 1/2: Flat silver tinsel.
Middle hackle: Grey squirrel tail hair.
Body front 1/2: Black fur dubbing.
Wings: Black-tipped woodchuck dyed orange or grey squirrel tail hair dyed orange.
Front hackle: Dyed yellow hair.

Hairy Black Practitioner

Hook: Single: Partridge CS10/1 Bartleet, Mustad 80500BL sizes 1/0-6.
Double: Partridge Q, Mustad 80525BL, Daiichi 7131 sizes 4-12.
Thread: Black 6/0 or 8/0.
Tag: Silver oval tinsel.
Antennae: 4 strands of pearl crystal hair.
Tail: First hackle: Black bucktail or other black hair. Second hackle: Grey squirrel dyed red.
Eyes: Red burnt nylon monofilament.
Ribbing: Oval silver tinsel over whole body.
Body rear 1/2: Black fur dubbing.
Rear wing: Black squirrel tail hair.
Middle hackle: Dyed black hair.
Body front 1/2: Black fur dubbing.
Front wing: Black squirrel tail hair.
Head hackle: Dyed black squirrel tail hair.
Head: Black varnish.

Practitioners

Hairy Ally's Practitioner

Hook: Single: Partridge CS10/1 Bartleet, Mustad 80500BL sizes 1/0-6.
Double: Partridge Q, Mustad 80525BL, Daiichi 7131, sizes 4-12.
Thread: Red or orange 6/0 or 8/0.
Tag: Gold oval tinsel.
Antennae: 4 strands of pearl crystal hair.
Tail: First hackle: Dyed orange bucktail or other orange hair.
Second hackle: Dyed red hair.
Eyes: Black burnt nylon monofilament.
Ribbing: Oval gold tinsel over whole body.
Body rear 1/2: Red fur dubbing.
Rear wing: Grey squirrel dyed hot orange.
Middle hackle: Grey squirrel tail hair.
Body front 1/2: Black fur dubbing.
Front hackle: Dyed orange hair.
Head: Red varnish.

Hairy Black and Silver Practitioner

Hook: Single: Partridge CS 10/1 Bartleet, Mustad 80500BL sizes 1/0-6.
Double: Partridge Q, Mustad 80525 BL Daiichi 7131 sizes 4-12.
Thread: Black 6/0 or 8/0.
Tag: Silver oval tinsel.
Antennae: 4 strands of pearl crystal hair.
Tail: First hackle: Grey squirrel tail hair dyed red. Second hackle: Black squirrel tail hair.
Eyes: Red burnt nylon monofilament.
Ribbing: None.
Body rear 1/2: Flat silver Mylar braid.
Rear wing: Black-tipped grey fox hair.
Middle hackle: Grey squirrel tail hair.
Body front 1/2: Flat silver Mylar braid.
Front wing: Black-tipped grey fox hair.
Head hackle: Black squirrel tail hair.
Head: Black varnish.

Hairy Cascade Practitioner

Hook: Single: Partridge CS10/1 Bartleet, Mustad 80500BL sizes 1/0-6.
Double: Partridge Q, Mustad 80525BL, Daiichi 7131 sizes 4-12.
Thread: Red or orange 6/0 or 8/0.
Tag: Silver oval tinsel.
Antennae: 4 strands of silver crystal hair.
Tail: First hackle: Mixture of yellow and orange bucktail or hair.
Second hackle: Dyed red hair.
Eyes: Black burnt nylon monofilament.

Ribbing: Oval silver tinsel over whole body.
Body rear 1/2: Flat silver tinsel.
Rear wing: Black squirrel hair with 2 strands of pearl crystal hair.
Middle hackle: Yellow hair.
Body front 1/2: Black fur dubbing.
Front wing: Black squirrel hair with 2 strands of pearl crystal hair.
Front hackle: Orange hair.
Head: Black varnish.

Hairy Highlander Practitioner

Hook: Single: Partridge BL10/1 Bartleet, Mustad 80500BL sizes 1/0-6.
Double: Partridge Q, Mustad 80525BL, Daiichi 7131 sizes 4-12.
Thread: Yellow 6/0 or 8/0.
Tag: Oval silver tinsel.
Antennae: 4 strands of pearl crystal hair.
Tail: First hackle: Dyed yellow hair.
Second hackle: Black-tipped opossum guard hairs.
Eyes: Black burnt nylon monofilament.
Ribbing: Oval gold tinsel over whole body.

Body rear 1/2: Bright yellow fur dubbing.
Rear wing: Grey squirrel hair dyed orange.
Middle hackle: Dyed green highlander hair.
Body front 1/2: Green highlander fur dubbing.
Front wing: Mixture of dyed yellow and green grey squirrel hair.
Head hackle: Yellow hair.
Head: Black varnish.

Hairy General Practitioner

Hook: Single: Partridge CS10/1 Bartleet, Mustad 80500BL sizes 1/0-6.
Double: Partridge Q, Mustad 80525 BL, Daiichi 7131 sizes 4-12.
Thread: Orange 6/0 or 8/0.
Tag: Oval gold tinsel.
Antennae: 4 strands of pearl crystal hair.
Tail: First hackle: Orange bucktail or hair.
Second hackle: Red hair.
Eyes: Black burnt nylon monofilament.

Ribbing: Gold oval tinsel over whole body.
Body rear 1/2: Orange fur dubbing.
Rear wing: Grey squirrel hair dyed red.
Middle hackle: Orange hair.
Body front 1/2: Orange fur dubbing.
Front wing: Grey squirrel hair dyed red.
Head hackle: Orange hair.
Head: Red varnish.

Hairy Purple Practitioner

Hook: Single: Partridge CS10/1 Bartleet, Mustad 80500BL sizes 1/0-6.
Double: Partridge Q, Mustad 80525BL, Daiichi 7131 sizes 4-12.
Thread: Black 6/0 or 8/0.
Tag: Oval silver tinsel.
Antennae: 4 strands of pearl crystal hair.
Tail: First hackle: Grey squirrel hair dyed purple.
Second hackle: Grey squirrel dyed red.
Eyes: Black burnt nylon monofilament.

Ribbing: Oval silver tinsel over whole body.
Body rear 1/2: Flat pearl tinsel.
Rear wing: Grey squirrel hair dyed purple.
Middle hackle: Natural grey squirrel hair.
Body front 1/2: Purple fur dubbing.
Front wing: Grey squirrel hair dyed purple.
Head hackle: Dyed purple grey squirrel hair.
Head: Black varnish.

Hairy Olive Practitioner

Hook: Single: Partridge CS10/1 Bartleet, Mustad 80500BL sizes 1/0-6.
Double: Partridge Q, Mustad 80525, Daiichi 7131 sizes 4-12.
Thread: Yellow 6/0 or 8/0.
Tag: Oval gold tinsel.
Antennae: 4 strands of pearl crystal hair.
Tail: First hackle: Grey squirrel hair dyed medium olive.
Second hackle: Grey squirrel hair dyed red.
Eyes: Black burnt nylon monofilament.
Ribbing: Oval gold tinsel over whole body.
Body rear 1/2: Fluorescent green fur dubbing.
Rear wing: Grey squirrel hair dyed medium olive.
Middle hackle: Fluorescent green hair.
Body front 1/2: Green olive fur dubbing.
Front wing: Grey squirrel dyed medium olive.
Head hackle: Olive hair.
Head: Black varnish.

Hairy Solduc Practitioner

Hook: Single: Partridge CS10/1 sizes 1-8. Double: Partridge Q, sizes 2-12.
Thread: Orange or yellow 6/0 or 8/0.
Tag: Oval silver tinsel.
Antennae: 4 strands of pearl crystal hair.
Tail: First hackle: Grey squirrel hair dyed yellow.
Second hackle: Dyed orange hair.
Eyes: Black mono eyes.
Ribbing: Oval silver tinsel.
Body: Rear half: Fluorescent orange dubbing.
Rear wing: Dyed orange hair.
Middle hackle: Yellow hair.
Body front 1/2: Hot orange dubbing.
Front wing: Grey squirrel tail dyed orange.
Head hackle: Black hair.
Head: Red lacquer.

Hairy Pink Practitioner

Hook: Single: Partridge CS10/1 Bartleet, Mustad 80500BL sizes 1/0-6.
Double: Partridge Q, Mustad 80525BL, Daiichi 7131, sizes 4-12.
Thread: Red 6/0 or 8/0.
Tag: Silver oval tinsel.
Antennae: 4 strands of pearl crystal hair.
Tail: First hackle: Pink bucktail or hair.
Second hackle: Grey squirrel hair bleached to a light ginger.
Eyes: Black burnt nylon monofilament.
Ribbing: Silver oval tinsel over whole body.
Body rear 1/2: Pink fur dubbing.
Rear wing: Squirrel tail bleached and dyed pink.
Middle hackle: Grey squirrel bleached to a light ginger with white tip.
Body front 1/2: Pink fur dubbing.
Front wing: Squirrel bleached and dyed pink.
Head hackle: Grey squirrel bleached to light ginger with white tip.
Head: Red varnish.

Hairy Durham Ranger Practitioner

Hook: Single: Partridge CS10/1 Bartleet, Mustad 80500BL sizes 1/0-6.
Double: Partridge Q, Mustad 80525BL, Daiichi 7131 sizes 4-12.
Thread: Orange 6/0 or 8/0.
Tag: Oval silver tinsel.
Antennae: 4 strands of pear crystal hair.
Tail: First hackle: Yellow bucktail or hair.
Second hackle: Dyed red hair.
Eyes: Black burnt nylon monofilament.
Ribbing: Oval silver tinsel over whole body.
Body rear half: 1/2 yellow fur dubbing, 1/2 orange fur dubbing.
Rear wing: Natural grey squirrel tail hair.
Middle hackle: Orange hair.
Body front half: 1/2 fiery brown fur dubbing, 1/2 black fur dubbing.
Front wing: Grey squirrel hair dyed orange.
Head hackle: Dyed blue hair.
Head: Black varnish.

Hairy Yellow Ally's Practitioner

Hook: Single: Partridge CS10/1 Bartleet, Mustad 80500BL sizes 1/0-6. Double: Partridge Q, Mustad 80525BL, Daiichi 7131 sizes 4-12.

Thread: Black 6/0 or 8//0.

Tag: Oval silver tinsel.

Antennae: 4 strands of pearl crystal hair.

Tail: First hackle: Yellow bucktail or hair. Second hackle: Golden olive hair.

Eyes: Black burnt nylon monofilament.

Ribbing: Silver oval tinsel over whole body.

Body rear 1/2: Flat silver tinsel or silver Mylar braid.

Rear wing: Grey squirrel dyed orange.

Middle hackle: Natural grey squirrel hair.

Body front 1/2: Black fur dubbing.

Front wing: Grey squirrel hair dyed orange.

Head hackle: Yellow hair.

Head: Black varnish.

Hairy Wintergreen Practitioner

Hook: Single: Partridge CS10/1 Bartleet, Mustad 80500BL sizes 1/0-6. Double: Partridge Q, Mustad 80525BL, Daiichi 7131 sizes 4 -12.

Thread: Yellow or olive 6/0 or 8/0.

Tag: Oval silver tinsel.

Antennae: 4 strands of pearl crystal hair.

Tail: First hackle: Orange bucktail or hair. Second: hackle: Grey squirrel hair dyed yellow.

Eyes: Black burnt nylon monofilament.

Ribbing: Oval silver tinsel over whole body.

Body rear 1/2: Silver Mylar braid.

Rear wing: Grey squirrel dyed green.

Middle hackle: Yellow hair.

Body front 1/2: Green olive fur dubbing.

Front wing: Grey squirrel hair dyed green.

Head hackle: Squirrel hair dyed olive.

Head: Olive or green varnish.

Hairy Bass Flies and Bugs

Hairy Yellow Practitioner

Hook: Single: Partridge CS10/1 Bartleet, Mustad 80500BL sizes 1/0-6. Double: Partridge Q, Mustad 80525BL, Daiichi 7131 sizes 4-12.

Thread: Yellow 6/0 or 8/0.

Tag: Silver oval tinsel.

Antennae: 4 strands of pearl crystal hair.

Tail: First hackle: Yellow bucktail or hair. Second hackle: Golden olive hair.

Eyes: Black burnt nylon monofilament.

Ribbing: Silver oval over whole body.

Body rear 1/2: Flat silver tinsel or silver Mylar braid.

Rear wing: Grey squirrel tail hair dyed yellow.

Middle hackle: Natural grey squirrel hair.

Body front 1/2: Black fur dubbing.

Front wing: Grey squirrel hair dyed yellow.

Head hackle: Yellow hair.

Head: Red varnish.

Hairy Olive Damsel Nymph

Hook: Any 2x-long nymph hook wtd. Your choice.

Thread: Dark green 6/0.

Weight: Copper or lead wire.

Eyes: Mono nymph eyes painted black.

Tail: Olive arctic fox fur "hair hackle" segmented with tying thread.

Thorax: Olive fur dubbing.

Hackle: Dyed olive arctic fox tail fibres.

Head: Brown dubbing.

Hairy Black Hairy Fairy

Hook: Partridge D4A, Mustad 9671, TMC 5262, Daiichi 1710 Bass sizes 2 and 4 wtd.: Trout sizes 6-10 wtd.
Thread: Black 6/0 or 8/0.
Under body: Black floss.
Weight: Lead or copper wire (keel on top of shank).

Tail: Black squirrel tail hair.
Body: Black fur dubbing brush.
Body hackle: Preformed black squirrel tail hair.
Head hackle: Black squirrel tail hair.

Hairy Olive Hairy Fairy

Hook: Partridge D4A, Mustad 9671, TMC 5262, Daiichi 1710. Bass sizes 2 and 4 wtd.: Trout sizes 6-10 wtd.
Thread: Yellow or olive 6/0 or 8/0.
Under body: Green or olive floss.
Weight: Lead or copper wire (keel on top of shank).

Tail: Grey squirrel tail hair dyed olive.
Body: Olive fur dubbing brush.
Body hackle: Preformed olive dyed grey squirrel tail hair.
Head hackle: Olive hair.

Hairy Brown Hairy Fairy

Hook: Partridge D4A, Mustad 9671, TMC5262, Daiichi 1710. Bass sizes 2 and 4 wtd.: Trout sizes 6-10 wtd.
Thread: Orange 6/0 or 8/0.
Under body: Brown or orange floss.
Weight: Lead or copper wire (keel on top of shank).

Tail: Red fox squirrel tail hair.
Body: Brown fur dubbing brush.
Body hackle: Preformed red fox squirrel tail hair.
Head hackle: Red fox tail hair.

Hairy Mouse

Hook: TMC 8089, Mustad 80300BR, Daiichi 2720 sizes 2-10.
Thread: Black or yellow 6/0.
Tail support: A 25-pound monofilament loop.
Tail: Black or brown leather strip 2 1/2 times the length of the hook's shank tapered from 3/16 inch at the base to 3/32 inch at the tip of the tail.

Body: A premade "hair hackle" of natural grey/brown deer hair.
Ears: A pair of shaped leather ears.
Head: Spun or stacked natural deer hair cut to shape.
Eyes: Black plastic beads cut in half.
Whiskers: Black squirrel tail hairs.
Weed guard: Very thin tungsten wire loop performed to the correct length.

Hairy Damsel Fly (Spent Style)

Hook: Preferred Partridge 01 sizes 6-12. Similar sizes in TMC 8089, Mustad 80300BR or Daiichi 2720

Thread: Black 6/0.

Eyes: Mono nymph eyes painted black.

Body: Dyed blue deer hair or bucktail.

Ribbing: Black tying thread.

Wings: Dyed grey deer hair with a few dyed blue deer-hair fibres mixed in.

Thorax: Dubbing brush of dyed-blue deer hair trimmed to shape.

Hackle: Sparse black squirrel tail.

Head: Black dubbing.

Hairy Olive Crayfish

Hook: Partridge D4A, Mustad 9671, TMC 5262, Daiichi 1710. Bass sizes 2 and 4 wtd.: Trout sizes 6-10 wtd.

Thread: Yellow or olive 6/0 or 8/0.

Under body: Green or olive floss.

Weight: Lead or copper wire (keel on top of shank).

Tail: Grey squirrel tail hair dyed olive.

Body: Olive fur dubbing brush.

Body hackle: Preformed olive dyed grey squirrel tail hair.

Head hackle: Olive hair.

Hairy Brown Crayfish

Hook: Partridge N, Mustad 90240, TMC 7989, Daiichi 2421 sizes 2-6 wtd.

Thread: Colour to blend with body material.

Under body: Floss silk to build up thorax slightly.

Weight: Lead or copper wire.

Antennae: Fine black bucktail or elk mane.

Nose: Short, fairly thick "hair hackle" of dyed fiery brown squirrel tail.

Eyes: 30-pound melted monofilament dipped in black varnish to make stalk eyes.

Claws: "Hair Hackle" of dyed brown opossum or raccoon fur.

Ribbing: Clear monofilament.

Thorax hackle: Woodchuck guard hairs dyed fiery brown.

Thorax: Ginger fur dubbing.

Abdomen: Ginger fur dubbing.

Carapce: Fox squirrel tail dyed fiery brown coated with softex and epoxy.

Tail: The butt ends of the carapace coated with Softex.

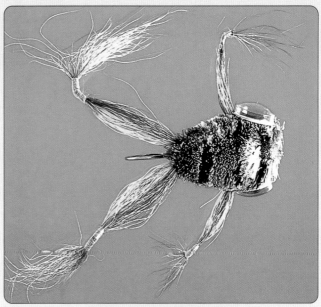

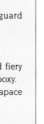

Hairy Frog (Weedless)

Hook: TMC 8089, Mustad 80300BR, Daiichi 2720 sizes 2-10.

Thread: Yellow 6/0 for legs and 4/0 for tying deer hair.

Hind legs: Yellow bucktail "hair hackle" followed by olive bucktail "hair hackle" divided and jointed.

Body: Black, yellow and olive deer hair stacked over yellow and white deer hair trimmed to shape.

Front legs: Yellow bucktail "hair hackle" followed by olive bucktail "hair hackle" divided jointed.

Head: Black, yellow and olive deer hair stacked over white deer hair trimmed to shape.

Eyes: Solid plastic eyes.

Weed guard: Thin stainless steel or tungsten wire loop.

Hairy Diving Bass Fry

Hook: Partridge N, Mustad 90240, TMC 7989, Daiichi 2421, sizes 1/0-4.
Thread: Yellow 4/0 or 6/0.
Under body: Cigar-shaped tapered body of floss silk with strip of lead wire under and a strand of monofilament either side of the shank.
Tail: Green olive 90%, and yellow 10% dyed grey squirrel tail hairs.
Ribbing: Clear monofilament.
Matuka back hackle: Preformed of rabbit fur dyed dark green and green deer hair.

Body: Mixture of 70% cream and 30% bright yellow fur made into a dubbing brush.
Pectoral fins: Grey squirrel tail hair dyed olive.
Gills: Dyed red rabbit fur.
Collar: Green over black deer hair stacked over mixture of white and yellow deer hair.
Head: Green over black deer hair stacked over white deer hair cut to shape and well varnished.
Eyes: Gold solid plastic doll's eyes.

Hairy Olive Fork-tailed Gerbubble Bug

Hook: TMC 8089, Mustad 80300BR, Daiichi 2720 sizes 2/0-10.
Thread: Green or olive 4/0 or 6/0.
Tail: Long dyed-olive fox hair or dyed-olive goat hair.
Collar: Dyed-olive black-tipped opossum hair.

Body side hackles: Preformed dyed-olive opossum hair.
Body: Olive stacked over golden olive deer hair.
Head: Dyed-orange deer hair.
Eyes: Plastic doll's eyes

Hairy Black Fork-tailed Gerbubble Bug

Hook: TMC8089, Mustad 80300BR, Daiichi 2720 sizes 2/0-10.
Thread: Black 4/0 or 6/0.
Tail: Dyed black fox fur (long fibred) or dyed-black goat hair.
Collar: Dyed black fox fur.
Body side hackles: Preformed natural black-tipped grey fox tail.

Underbody: Two lengths of 50-pound monofilament tied on either side of the hook shank to widen the body.
Body: Black stacked over grey deer hair body hair.
Head: Dyed red deer hair body hair.
Weed guard: "U"-shaped stainless steel wire.
Eyes: Plastic doll's eyes

Hairy Pink Fork-tailed Gerbubble Bug

Hook: TMC8089, Mustad 80300BR, Daiichi 2720 sizes 2/0-10.
Thread: Red 4/0 or 6/0.
Tail: Long dyed-cerise fox hair or dyed-cerise goat hair.
Collar: Pink hair.

Body side hackles: Preformed dyed-pink hair.
Body: Cerise stacked over pink deer hair.
Head: Dyed-red deer hair.
Eyes: Plastic doll's eyes

Hairy Yellow Fork-tailed Gerbubble Bug

Hook: TMC 8089, Mustad 80300BR, Daiichi 2720 sizes 2/0-10.
Thread: Yellow 4/0 or 6/0.
Tail: Long dyed-yellow fox hair or dyed-yellow goat hair.
Collar: Yellow hair.

Body side hackles: Woodchuck guard hairs dyed yellow.
Body: Yellow stacked over pale yellow deer hair.
Head: Dyed-red deer hair.
Eyes: Plastic doll's eyes

Index

Hair-Hackle Tying Techniques & Fly Patterns

Directory of Material Suppliers

U.K. Retailers

Angling Pursuits (Peter Scott)
Old Drumchapel,
Glasgow, G15 6PB, Scotland
Tel. 0141 944 7658

Cookhill Fly Tying (Steve Cooper)
"M" Holding, Roughcote Lane
Caverswall, Stoke-on Trent
ST11 9ES, England
Tel. 01782 388 382

D.J. Hackle
Manbys Farm, Oaksey
Malmesbury, Wiltshire
SN16 9TG, England
Tel. 01666 577 399

Farlows of Pall Mall
5 Pall Mall, London
SW1Y 5NP, England
Tel. 020 7839 8959

Ellis Slater
47 Bridgecross Road
Chase Terrace, Burntwood
Staff., WS7 8 BU, England
Tel. 01543 671377

Rutland Fishing
7 St. Pauls Street, Stamford
Linc., PE9 2BE, England
Tel. 01780 482 901

U.K. Wholesalers

Gordon Griffiths Fishing Tackle
Unit 1/8, Lifford Way
Binley Industrial Estate
Coventry, CV3 2RN, England
Tel. 02476 440 859

Lureflash Internatonal Ltd.
Victoria Buildings, Victoria Street
Kilnhurst, Maxborough
South Yorkshire, S64 5SQ
England
Tel. 01709 580 238

Medway Feather Co
Brasenose Road
Gillingham, ME74 4JR, England
Tel. 01634 852 841

Scotia Complete
136 Victoria Street
Dyce, Aberdeen
AD2 0BE Scotland
Tel. 01224 722253

USA Suppliers

Blue Ribbon Flies
P.O. Box 1037, 309 Canyon Street
West Yellowstone, MT. 59758
Tel. 406/646-7643

Keough Hackles
(For Gordon Griffiths Fishing Tackle)
23392 Hwy. M. 60
Menton, MI 49072
Tel. 877/496-7478

Whitetail Fly Tying Supplies
7060 Whitetail Court
Toledo, OH 43617
Tel. 419/843-2106

Rocky Mountain Dubbing
P.O. Box 1255, 115 Poppy Street
Lander, WY 82420
Tel. 307/332-2989

Spirit River Inc.
423 Winchester Street
Roseburg, OR 97470
Tel. 541/440-6916

Umpqua Feather Merchants,
17537 N. Umpqua Highway
P.O. Box 700
Glide, OR 97443
Tel. 541/496-3512

White Fox Fur & Feather Co.
226 Main Street
P.O. Box 3
Pemberton MN 56078-0003
Tel. 507/869-3877